KINGS & QUEENS

OF EMPIRE

British Monarchs 1760-2000

KINGS & QUEENS
OF EMPIRE
British Monarchs 1760-2000

J.M. Golby & A.W. Purdue

TEMPUS

First published as *The Monarchy and the British People* in 1988 by B.T. Batsford Ltd
Revised illustrated edition published 2000

PUBLISHED IN THE UNITED KINGDOM BY:

Tempus Publishing Ltd
The Mill, Brimscombe Port
Stroud, Gloucestershire GL5 2QG

PUBLISHED IN THE UNITED STATES OF AMERICA BY:

Tempus Publishing Inc.
2 Cumberland Street
Charleston, SC 29401

Tempus books are available in France, Germany and Belgium
from the following addresses:

Tempus Publishing Group	Tempus Publishing Group	Tempus Publishing Group
21 Avenue de la République	Gustav-Adolf-Straße 3	Place de L'Alma 4/5
37300 Joué-lès-Tours	99084 Erfurt	1200 Brussels
FRANCE	GERMANY	BELGIUM

British Library Cataloguing in Publication Data.
A catalogue record for this book is available from the British Library.

ISBN 0 7524 1775 4

Typesetting and origination by Tempus Publishing.
PRINTED AND BOUND IN GREAT BRITAIN.

Contents

Acknowledgements

The authors and publishers wish to thank the following for permission to reproduce paintings and illustrations: Brighton Corporation (p.35); The British Museum (p.37); Neville Elder (p.133); Her Majesty the Queen (p.18. p.19, p.44, p.72, p.87); The Mansell Collection (p.28); The National Portrait Gallery (p.73, p.102, p.129).

List of illustrations

Introduction

Most people when they read that the Queen walked on the slopes at Windsor – that the Prince of Wales went to the Derby – have imagined that too much thought and prominence were given to little things. But they have been in error...
(Walter Bagehot, *The English Constitution*, 1867)

Writing in 1937, soon after Edward VIII had given up the throne to marry Mrs Wallis Simpson, an American observer resident in this country pointed out two apparent paradoxes concerning the British monarchy and British society. First, although supposedly a democracy, there was no other country where Royalty occupied so large a part in the public and private lives of the people and where the Royal Family was such an 'object of adulation, adoration and sentimentality'. Second, although the British monarch possessed virtually no political powers and, at least in the case of Edward VIII, could not even choose a wife without the consent of the Prime Minister, the monarch did exert a huge 'influence over the minds and social life of a great portion of the people'.[1] Indeed, in the view of the writer, the social influence of the British monarchy on the nation was greater than any dictator in Europe could exert upon his own country.

Sixty years later, even a casual viewing of television and newspapers and a stroll around bookshops and magazine stores may well confirm these views. While very few people in Britain believe that, compared with politicians, business institutions, trade unions, the media and even the church, the monarchy wields any real political power, there is little doubt that the actions and behaviour of members of the royal family are followed just as closely, if not more so, than those of politicians, pop stars and other celebrities. Individual members of the royal family frequently, and for a variety of reasons, come under severe criticism from the media; public opinion may be split over which partner was most responsible for the break-up of a marriage, and debates may take place within the country about the future or of the need for the monarchy, nevertheless the thousands of people who line the streets for royal ceremonies and the millions who view each royal occasion on television, and who avidly read about the life styles of the various members of the Royal Family, testify to the wide extent of popular support for the monarchy existing within the country. Even those who profess little interest in, or are even sceptical about, the institution, very often have had their attitudes altered, if only temporarily, after coming into contact with the monarchy. Certainly, over the last two hundred years, many politicians of the left have started their careers by criticizing the institution and ended by praising it. George Orwell, no great admirer of the monarchy, nevertheless admitted that the Royal Family exerted some sort of compelling attraction. Writing in 1947 in *Tribune* he observed that during his lifetime, 'on only two occasions did I feel, at the time, that I was seeing something significant'. One of these was when he witnessed Queen Mary

Why is it that at times of celebration crowds congregate outside Buckingham Palace? Celebrating victory, 1918.

travelling in a royal coach.

> One day I was walking past Windsor Castle when a sort of electric shock seemed to go through the street. People were taking their hats off, soldiers springing to attention. And then, clattering over the cobbles, there came a huge, plum-coloured open carriage drawn by four horses with postilions... Even at that date (1920 or thereabouts) it gave me a wonderful feeling of looking backwards through a window into the nineteenth century.[2]

Just why the Royal Family arouses so much interest and emotion is a question which has attracted the attention of many sociologists. Some have concluded that the Royal Family are merely the object of various fantasies and identifications, just as pop stars and other mass entertainers are regarded. Others, however, endow the interest in the monarchy and its functions with much more deep-rooted motivations, both secular and sacred. By her participation as leader in state occasions and other rituals, the Queen fulfils a deep-seated need within society to reflect and reaffirm a number of strongly held national and moral values and, it has been argued, the centrality of this role in reflecting social integration and national unity is similar to that performed in the past by the medieval church. An alternative interpretation is much less mystical and sees the monarch's popularity and role in promoting national unity and moral consensus as one which is used by the ruling elite for its own purposes, harnessing these qualities in order to 'guarantee the legitimacy of the existing social and property order' and to reduce antagonisms towards their own political authority. Indeed, to consolidate their own dominance they exploit 'pageantry as propaganda'.[3]

Yet, however interesting these theories may be and however valid they may seem at any particular time, they are unable to account for the many changes that have taken place over recent centuries with regard to the standing and relationship of the monarchy to the nation, and the varying extent to which the monarchy has exerted a social influence over its subjects. The Queen and members of the Royal Family may nowadays be willing to go on walkabouts and shake the hands of their subjects, but in no way is this represented as anything other than an attempt to remove the more formal and awesome barriers existing between the monarch and her subjects. In contrast, in the seventeenth century, the acts of touching, being touched by, or possessing something touched by the monarch, carried with them a belief in miraculous healing powers. Charles II, for example, claimed to possess the royal touch which could cure the King's Evil and he exercised it on over 100,000 of his subjects at considerable expense, for £49,000 was spent by him on gold touch pieces. When George I and George II refused to continue this royal tradition, they inevitably reduced the esteem in which the monarchy was held, for many of the public.

Again, although the Queen is nominally the head of the Church of England, there is no suggestion that she possesses any divine right, a concept which although shaken by the events of 1688-89 and 1714-15, had not been totally destroyed during the reigns of the early Hanoverians. Indeed, the reason for the continued appeal of the Stuart cause lay in its identification with a religious, mystical and charismatic concept of monarchy. Jacobites argued for the divine status of monarchy and the accountability of kings to God alone; they claimed that the Crown could only descend by indefeasible hereditary right and pointed to the scriptural injunctions to obedience to divinely appointed kings. Recent research has established that Jacobitism remained a potent force until the 1750s and, far from being confined to the fringes of the realm, could be found in thriving centres of commerce and in London itself. If such beliefs found a following among aristocrats, gentry and merchants, how much stronger they must have been, albeit in cruder form, among the lower orders and in popular culture. Here magic and superstition remained potent and kings could be seen as not just enjoying divine right but as being semi-divine themselves. As J.C.D. Clark has remarked, 'too little weight is often given to the immense continuity, the vast inertia, of popular and rural sentiment'.[4]

One reason often given for the popularity of the present monarch is that she exercises little political power or, as it is often put, is above politics, and therefore she is not subject to the hostility that is invariably shown by some sections of the population towards those who wield power. But the idea of the monarch being above politics is a relatively recent one. The early Hanoverians exercised formidable personal political powers. George I maintained almost complete control in foreign affairs and military matters, while he reserved to himself the granting of peerages and honours together with the appointment of bishops. Nothing, in fact, so graphically illustrates the power of the monarchy in the

PUNCH'S PENCILLINGS.—N⁰. IX.

THE ROYAL RED RIDING HOOD,
AND THE MINISTERIAL WOLF.

The political influence of the monarchy. As late as 1841 the monarchy could be seen as politically partisan and possessed of the means of political persuasion. This Punch *cartoon of September 1841 depicts Queen Victoria as the person who could bestow 'Place, Patronage, Power, Perquisites and Pensions'.*

eighteenth century as the tendency, indeed the necessity, for political opposition factions to cluster around the reversionary interest of the heir to the throne. The dissension between George II and his eldest son went beyond even the customary mutual distaste and suspicion that characterized the relations between kings and heirs in the House of Hanover. Frederick's home, Leicester House, was the haunt of disaffected Whigs and non-Jacobite Tories. Thirty years later it was George III's eldest son, the Prince of Wales, who provided the focus for opposition politicians. Even in the early nineteenth century the political power of the monarch was such that both George IV and William IV were in positions to interfere with and ultimately dismiss administrations. The young Queen Victoria also clearly showed her interest in politics and, in particular, her preference for the Whig party. In this respect, in 1839, she played an important part in ensuring the prolongation of the Whig ministry led by her favourite, Lord Melbourne.[5]

Nevertheless, the political power of the monarchy has gradually been reduced and it can well be argued that it is only because the British monarchy has gracefully withdrawn from a politically active role that it has survived. The word 'survived' suggests that the institution has, at least at times, been under severe pressure and attack, but compared with

A Gordons Gin advertsisement at the time of George VI's Coronation. Even if a royal appointment was not obtained, firms attempted to associate themselves with royal tradition at times of celebration.

most other European royal families, this has not been the case. The last 150 years has been a disastrous period for many European monarchies. Even if the minor royal houses of the German and Italian principalities are excluded, since 1848 fourteen monarchies have been deposed in Europe. In Britain, however, the Royal Family has not merely survived, it has secured a position where, especially in troubled times, it unites the nation. Indeed, not only does the monarchy unite the nation, but in a world context, and certainly since 1945 as the international prestige of the country has declined, it is only at the time of major royal occasions that the rest of the world turns its eyes towards Britain. The wedding of Prince Charles to Lady Diana Spencer in 1981 was of such worldwide interest that, with the involvement of 109 television broadcasting organizations, an estimated 750 million people in seventy-four countries were enabled to watch the wedding.[6] Princess Diana's funeral was also an international event.

Connected with this is the role the monarchy now plays in the economy of the country. Very soon after the start of our period special plates, cups and mugs commemorating royal events were produced.[7] By the time of Edward VII's coronation not only was there a much wider range of commemorative memorabilia but London itself was crowded with visitors from abroad intent on witnessing the ceremonies. By the time of Prince Charles's wedding, London hotels were crammed, theatres in the evenings were fully booked and the commercial possibilities of the event were exploited to the full, so that all manner of goods commemorating the wedding filled department stores and street markets alike.

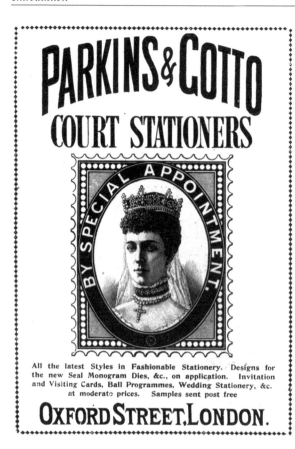

A royal association, real or imaginary, has always helped sales, though this direct appeal would not be permitted today.

The appearance and the participation of the Royal Family in ceremonies and state rituals do help to focus world attention, however fleetingly, on Britain, and in addition stimulate all sorts of commercial opportunities. No doubt these events, together with their roles as patrons of numerous charitable institutions, also underline the role of the Royal Family in bolstering traditions, continuity and national unity. But their activities throughout the year, both as individuals and as members of a family, also influence to a greater or lesser degree the habits, manners, morals, fashions and tastes of the nation. Whether it be in representing, if not reinforcing, moral values relating to the virtues of family life, or just the transmission of a transitory fashion such as a Princess Di hair-do, there is no doubting the close and interactive relationship between the Royal Family and British society, or what the American observer in 1937 called the influencing of 'the minds and social life of a great portion of the people'.

A basic element in the enduring appeal of the monarchy is, though it might seem a disadvantage in an ostentatiously democratic age, that it is a hereditary and therefore a family system. Presidential families may increase or detract from electoral appeal but they depart from the public stage as presidents leave office, whereas marriage, birth and relationship are the very stuff of monarchy. 'A family on the throne,' wrote Walter Bagehot, 'is an interesting idea also. It brings down the pride of sovereignty to the level of petty life… The Women – one half the human race at least – care fifty times more for a

The Cup Final, 1939. Sporting events are often occasions where the monarchy and working people find common ground.

marriage than a ministry.'[8] The truth of Bagehot's comment confounds its cynicism, for 'the Women' are, of course, correct in their priorities. Whereas elective office is mechanistic and temporary, a 'family on the throne' is an organic element which binds together past and present and provides not only an icon of national unity but a number of models and occasions for personal identification.

The aim of this book is to explore how, as the political power of the monarchy declined, its social influence was asserted and, from time to time, increased. In order to do this, we have examined the manner in which successive monarchs have presented themselves to an ever-changing British public; the ways they have coped with particular political, public and private events; the use they have made of ceremonials and royal occasions; and the ways they have been represented in the press and by cartoonists and, in recent years, by radio and television. We have started the study with George III because, as has recently been pointed out, it was during his reign that the political power of the monarchy was 'less strongly asserted than before'.[9] George III and each successive monarch developed his or her own style and public image and not all have been equally successful. Sometimes, as in the case of George IV during the Queen Caroline affair, the low standing and the lack of influence the monarch possessed with the British public was entirely of his own making. At other times luck has played an important part. Longevity alone did much to raise

Victoria's popularity within the country during the last two decades of her reign. In the case of most of the monarchs, however, they have been acutely aware of their duties and the role they were being asked to assume. The role changes as society changes, but in the last resort it is not the personality of the particular monarch which holds sway with the public, but the institution. After all, the popular Edward VIII was very soon forgotten after his abdication. The institution is greater than the individual, and it is an institution whose present-day standing and presence very much derives from and depends upon its own past.

1 George III
The Father of his People

Whereas, seemingly, every appearance and speech of the Queen today is reported to the country at large, in 1760 George III's actions and deeds were not exposed to such communal examination. Indeed, his immediate context was that of the leader of a close-knit 'Society', and although he was at the apex of this social hierarchy, the leading members of society were as rich and lived in as grand a state as George himself. The difficulties of countrywide communications set limits upon the degree to which George could impress himself upon his subjects as a whole, and communication with them was usually confined to those immediately below him in the hierarchy. Of course, if faced with aristocratic faction or overmighty Whig grandees, the monarch did have the option of appealing to a wider society of gentry and merchants or, *in extremis*, even to their inferiors, but the great lesson that aristocracy and monarchy had learnt from the events of the Civil War was that of their mutual dependence and the desirability of keeping disputes within the bounds set by that dependence.

In 1760 the links between the monarchy and a wide section of the public were not characterized by warm loyalty or an awe of majesty. George II, a monarch whose love for his native Hanover caused him to put Hanoverian before British interests, could make little claim to be the father of his people. Compared with the romantic appeal of Jacobitism, which was identified with a religious, mystical and charismatic concept of monarchy, the early Hanoverians appeared equivocal about a monarchic tradition that they had half inherited and half appropriated. Considering these circumstances, George III's achievement during his reign, of identifying the monarchy with the nation and in creating new links between monarch and society, is a remarkable one.

There were a number of factors favourable to the consolidation and enhancement of the position of the Crown when George succeeded his grandfather to the throne in 1760. Extremely important was the fact that George III, unlike his Hanoverian and even Stuart predecessors, was untainted by 'abroad', by either birth, a period of exile, or even a taste for foreign alliances, all of which were repugnant to large sections of his subjects. George never even visited Hanover, although it is true that when he contemplated abdication in 1782 he considered retiring there. In an age when national pride and the feeling of the superiority of 'free-born Englishmen' to all things foreign was growing apace, this was a major asset. George's father had realized this and, although he had spent the first twenty years of his life in Germany, had thrown himself enthusiastically into the role of Englishman, even to the extent of taking up such national pastimes as cricket, dog-fighting and the breaking of other people's windows when drunk. But George could also lay claim to being *British*. He was advised to stress this by his Scottish teacher, the Earl of Bute, and in the short run it did George little good in England. For Bute in particular was seen as an insidious influence on George, and Scotsmen in general were regarded as a troublesome

George III on the terrace at Windsor, 1807, by Stroehling. The King is wearing the Windsor uniform he designed himself, a form of which is still worn today by the male members of the Royal Family when they are at Windsor. As men's dress became plainer in the late eighteenth century, uniforms became fashionable as a way of denting rank and position.

lot, concerned only to feather their nests at the expense of the richer partner in the Union. As the century wore on these prejudices were partly broken down and Englishmen, Welshmen and Scotsmen began, like George, to glory in the name of Britain. The success and valour of Scottish regiments played a part in making Scotland more popular in England and Wales and in making Scots identify with Britain, but the most important factor was the growing prosperity of the nation as a whole. The economy and cultural life of lowland Scotland throve under the Union and both Scotland and Wales, and particularly their landowning, commercial and professional classes, were steadily integrated within a British economy and culture.

A development which had little to do with George himself but which aided him in his successful attempt to reassert a continuity with previous dynasties and with long-established royal tradition, was the virtual demise of Jacobitism during this period. Jacobitism had contained political, quasi-religious and cultural dimensions and it rested, not only on personal loyalty to the Stuart dynasty, but on the old but still vital concept of kingship, which the early Hanoverians could only clumsily and inappropriately attempt to fulfil. The decline of Jacobitism therefore removed an obstacle and provided a new opportunity for the monarch to be perceived as a focus for unity rather than as a source of division. It allowed George to harness the monarchy's past to its present in a way that would have been difficult and dangerous for the first two Georges to attempt.

Indeed, if George's reign is crucial for the development of the monarchy, it is as much because of its re-affirmation and refurbishment of a role and an imagery of monarchy that expressed continuity with the past as for important innovations which pointed towards the monarchy of the future. This can be clearly seen in relation to the King's role and his

Queen Charlotte, c.1800, by Johann Zoffany. Despite the fact that the marriage of George III and Queen Charlotte was for many years a model of simple and intimate domesticity, the couple became increasingly estranged in later years.

position as head of the Church of England. Eighteenth-century Britain was a state in which the disabilities imposed on Dissenters and Roman Catholics were no mere anachronistic hangovers retained for quasi-political purposes; they were essential to a society which saw established religion as part of its identity and purpose.

There was more of a duality in the relations between church and government than a domination of one by the other. A deeply religious man, George was both humble and autocratic in his relations with the church. He took off the crown at his coronation while receiving communion, thereby signifying his humbleness before God, but equally he took the coronation oath to defend the Protestant faith with literal seriousness. He protected zealously his right to appoint bishops and defied Pitt when the latter proposed to introduce Catholic emancipation. In so doing he was in tune with the expectations and beliefs of the majority of his subjects: a Protestant king ruling by divine providence over a Protestant nation.

Historians, in their desire to trace emergent developments, have perhaps put too much emphasis on the new presentation of monarchy in the nineteenth century, seeing the invention of tradition when they are merely watching its repackaging and refurbishment.[1] The rituals and the public display of monarchy are modified and, to a degree, re-interpreted in every generation, but such are the fates of all ceremony and all rites of passage. The differences between George III's coronation and that of Elizabeth II are considerable but the differences pale beside the salient similarities. It is probably true that the mystic and religious significance of the former was more vital, immediate and literal to George's subjects, only a privileged few of whom witnessed the coronation, than to those who watched in their millions the crowning of Elizabeth, though even here the change may be exaggerated by the sociologists and historians who have diagnosed it for us.

A king is a king, according to the constitution, whether he has been crowned or not. He becomes king at the moment of the death of his predecessor. Yet the coronation is the public and religious affirmation of succession, and monarchs and subjects alike have seen crowning as the most important rite of monarchy. Coronations have always combined the religious and symbolic with the sheer might of majesty as expressed in the pomp and grandeur of the occasion. The balance between the two has, no doubt, changed over time but the most important change in this 'theatre of majesty' has been the size and nature of its audience. It has been argued that there was a Hanoverian hiatus between the great public ritual of Tudor and Stuart times and the staging of elaborate public pageantry for a mass society from the late nineteenth century onwards. Hanoverian royal ritual, it is argued, was for a narrow elite and failed 'to articulate a coherent ceremonial language' for there was 'no vocabulary of pageantry, no syntax of spectacle, no ritualistic idiom'.[2] Such a view almost certainly exaggerates the degree to which Stuart and Tudor pageantry was directed at an immediate public which extended beyond the elite. To impress a London crowd was certainly useful, but what was essential was the witness of the aristocracy; to subjects in general, to whom a king or queen was a symbolic rather than a real face, what was important was that the monarch had been crowned and anointed in the presence of the leaders of society.

It may well be the case that the narrow base of loyalty on which early Hanoverian monarchs rested made their coronations the concern of only a section of the elite, and less than convincing, even at a necessary distance, to the mass of their subjects. Yet the controversial nature of their right to succeed made the ritual crowning even more important. Although some expected the Stuart heir, Prince Charles Edward, to take up the gauntlet when the King's champion ceremonially hurled it down at the coronation banquet, George III's coronation took place in the context of an almost complete national consensus as to the legitimacy of the proceedings. His coronation was not professional theatre or organized with the precision and timing that comes from rehearsal and careful planning, but there is little reason to believe that it was less important both to its witnesses, and the wider public who heard about it, than the coronations of Stuart monarchs or George's successors.

Some aspects of George III's coronation made it appear very different from twentieth-century ones. The King and Queen made their way from St James's Palace to Westminster Hall in sedan chairs 'like ordinary citizens going to the theatre'.[3] There were no marching soldiers, for soldiers were not popular with London crowds in the eighteenth century, nor was it considered seemly for a king to go among his subjects protected by armed men. The coronation banquet in Westminster Hall, and the challenge from the King's champion to anyone who disputed George's right to the throne, were considered almost as important as the actual crowning in the Abbey; in view of the possibility that Prince Charles Edward might come forward, the challenge must indeed have been a highlight!

The proceedings were, as John Brooke has remarked, protracted:

> The procession set out for Westminster Hall at eleven in the morning but it was not until 1.30 that the King and Queen entered the Abbey and not until 3.30 that the King was crowned. Then came the coronation banquet and at 10 pm the King and Queen returned to St James's as they had set out.[4]

A few things went wrong. The sword of state was forgotten and the Lord Mayor's sword had to be borrowed instead. Also, the Lord High Steward's horse had been so well schooled in walking backwards for its exit that it did the same for its entrance, thus presenting its rump to the King and Queen. One biographer of George III later dismissed these mishaps as 'trifling incidents' and argued that 'by eighteenth century standards, the banquet was well organized';[5] but the King complained to the Deputy Earl Marshal and received the tactless reply: 'it is true, sir, that there has been some neglect, but I have taken care that the next coronation shall be regulated in the exactest manner possible'.[6]

Monarchy in the mid-eighteenth century addressed itself to 'Society' and through it to all its subjects; it did not seek to project itself to a wider society via a succession of elaborate state occasions or royal visits. George III was not a great traveller, and he never visited, nor saw the necessity of visiting, the north of England, Scotland, Wales or Ireland. The coronation was *sui generis* and not just the greatest of a number of royal spectacles; even on that occasion the actual proceedings were for the benefit of the bishops and the higher nobility. Ordinary Londoners, of course, would witness the coronation procession and there might be bonfires, free beer and even free beef in provincial towns, but for the most part the majority of the people were only vicariously involved.

Also, it is most unlikely that the inhabitants of Shropshire villages or Scottish provincial towns, who probably did not receive accounts of the coronation ceremony until weeks after the event, would have remarked on the standard of stage-management of the coronation or have been concerned about those minor lapses which did not involve mystical or prophetic implications. That the King had been properly crowned, anointed and acclaimed would be important to these people, while the fact that one of the largest jewels had fallen from the crown would be worried over and, after the loss of the American colonies, remembered as an omen.

George III combined an exemplary domestic life, emphasizing simplicity and economy, with a proper regard for the dignity of monarchy and its need to be grand and at times magnificent. In his concern for the latter he was severely handicapped, as indeed in his political aims, by the great mistake he made, on the advice of Bute, in accepting a woefully inadequate provision from the Civil List at the beginning of his reign. By declining to press for the generous provision accorded to George II, who had been granted the full hereditary revenue of the Crown, he put in jeopardy his financial and even political independence. He accepted a Civil List provision of £800,000, whereas if he had continued the existing arrangement he might well, on revenues which expanded with the national economy, have enjoyed an income of perhaps £2 million by the end of his reign. As it was he was perpetually in debt. Only a small portion of the Civil List, the Privy Purse, was for the monarch's private expenditure and George found himself having to support much of the necessary expense of government (the salaries of ministers, ambassadors and judges for instance) and then having to appeal to an often unsympathetic Parliament to pay off debts so incurred. Yet he did manage, to the nation's gain, to build and refurbish royal residences, to give royal patronage to the arts and sciences, to expand the honours system and to make the Crown more visible and more the property of the wider nation. Contemporary satirists and Whig historians pilloried variously his private parsimony, his necessary and traditional political expenditure and the extravagance of his sons, but few

This Gillray cartoon emphasizes the modest fare enjoyed by George and Charlotte, but also suggests that such frugality is disapproved of in royalty almost as much as is the wildest extravagance. The Queen's German background is lampooned in the sauerkraut she is eating.

TEMPERANCE *enjoying a Frugal Meal.*

sovereigns have got such good value out of straitened means. Indeed, despite the economies forced upon him, it has been estimated that during the course of his reign, when an increasing number of charitable foundations were being founded, George donated a larger percentage of his private income to various charities than any other British monarch.[7]

At a time when mighty subjects alternated between country seats and palaces and their magnificent town houses, it was necessary that royal residences should not be shoddy in comparison. George was not fond of London, breeding ground of the mobs which had insulted his mother and himself and then defied him during the anti-government riots of the 1760s, led by John Wilkes. Not surprisingly, he preferred to commute to London, first from Kew and later from Windsor. However, he did buy Buckingham House and, though St James's continued to be the residence of government, this became his London home. He added the castellated palace, designed by Wyatt, to the several small royal residences at Kew and began the extensive restoration of Windsor Castle. But his architectural schemes did not long outlast him. Kew Palace was pulled down and his alterations to Buckingham House and Windsor Castle were submerged in the more extensive and imaginative restorations of George IV, but they do demonstrate his concern that the Crown should have settings worthy of it.

If many anecdotes of George reveal him as an unpretentious man, fond of his domestic life, interested in farming, riding and hunting, and delighting in talking to ordinary subjects, he was ever conscious of the dignity of his position and realized how important

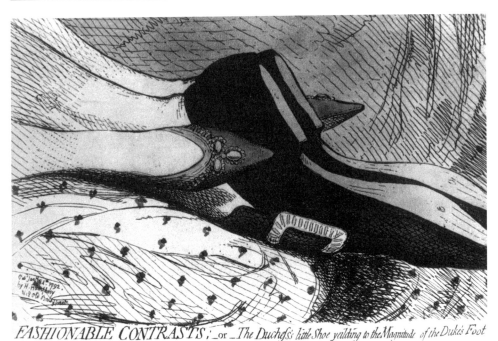

FASHIONABLE CONTRASTS ; – or – The Duchess's little Shoe yielding to the Magnitude of the Duke's Foot

A Gillray cartoon of 29 January 1792. The Duke of York's marriage in the previous year had been very popular and the Duchess's appearance and her dainty feet much admired. This cartoon enjoyed a revival at the time of the present Duke of York's marriage to Sarah Ferguson in 1986.

external trappings and etiquette were to it. His 'Farmer George' image did him much good with provincial and country opinion, but the ordinariness of monarchs is only interesting by contrast with their exalted position, and condescension can only work as a departure from a lofty height. George re-interpreted the state of royalty within the fashion of his period, more cautiously and modestly than many of his continental counterparts, but emphatically none the less. Honours exalt both the giver and the recipient and bind them together, and George revitalized the honours system, extending the Orders of the Bath and Garter and founding the Order of St Patrick. In his later years he even contemplated an order for females of distinction – a sure sign, contemporaries noted, of his madness! The Windsor uniform 'in blue and gold turned up with red' is another instance of his desire to give dignity and colour to the royal household.

In his patronage of the arts and of science, George took over where Charles II had left off. His appearance, bluff manner and staccato speech disguised not sensitivity or high intelligence, but a conscientious and persevering interest in books, music, science and the visual arts. He founded and endowed the Royal Academy, patronized the astrologer Herschel, furthered the botanic gardens at Kew, was an enthusiastic and experimental farmer, and collected an important private library of over 65,000 books which George IV later presented to the British Museum. The giving of the royal accolade to institutions, and royal patronage of facets of cultural life are traditions which subsequent monarchs were to extend, but George, if not an innovator, was here an important link between

The monarch as patron of the arts.King George and Queen Charlotte attend the theatre at Covent Garden.

Charles II and Prince Albert; he was surely wise in this as royal patronage in such areas spreads and diffuses royal influence into parts not reached by the patronage of courtiers and politicians.

As a politically active king, George's reputation and popularity were inevitably affected by the success or failure and the popularity or unpopularity of his ministers and their policies. George's association with Bute was undoubtedly damaging to him during the first years of his reign because Bute was both a political outsider and a maladroit and squeamish politician. Nevertheless, the reign began amid the euphoria of victory at the end of the Seven Years War – a euphoria which might have aided the popularity of the young monarch, except that George was seen as the enemy of the architect of victory and national hero, Pitt, and as the pawn of the peace party, which seemed to be throwing away the fruits of victory. The Wilkes affair and the failure, despite an expensive war, to retain the American colonies saw him lampooned by satirists and cartoonists and a target for the London mob. It is difficult to decide whether such unpopularity was general throughout the country or how George was regarded by Dorsetshire labourers or Northumbrian gentry, to say nothing of Scottish sentiment, and it may well have been confined to the metropolis and to some large towns. The ease of his victory in 1783 and 1784 over his political enemies reveals that when he appealed to a wider polity, over the heads of political factions, he obtained widespread support. The defeat of the Fox-North coalition does seem, however, to have been a turning point in his popularity and the eighties and nineties witnessed growing approbation and affection for the King.

Monarchs do, of course, tend to become more popular as they get older and in the younger Pitt the King found a capable and decisive first minister. One of the dominant political problems for much of his reign was the need and 'the quest for a minister who could command the confidence of both the crown and the House of Commons'.[8] The younger Pitt fulfilled this role. But the 'apotheosis' of George III, as Linda Colley has called the flowering of monarchist sentiment in late-eighteenth century Britain, stemmed also from wider developments.[9] One was the growth of patriotism in this period and the very appropriation of the word 'patriotism' to describe loyalty to the nation and to the monarchy. Wilkes had claimed to be a patriot and the term had often been used to describe those who were opposed to the monarchy and were in the tradition of political dissent or, though the word was not used at the time, 'radicalism'. A more united and prosperous country surviving a series of wars evolved a positive and nationalistic patriotism which identified the King as its focus and symbol. The threat from the French Revolution to Britain and its social and political status quo may have revealed weaknesses, manifested in the extent of radical reformist sentiment as expressed in Corresponding Societies and more proto-revolutionary organizations, and the degree to which radicalism could feed off economic discontent, but the weaknesses pale against the country's underlying strength. The winter of 1782-83 saw a remarkable outpouring of patriotic and loyalist feeling throughout the country, one expression of which was the formation of some 1,500 loyalist and 'Church and King' societies. These societies represent, it has been argued, 'the rallying of the propertied classes in defence of the throne, the church and the constitution. What they achieved, within their particular communities, was the mobilization of common people in defence of these institutions upon a wave of unprecedented sentiment'.[10]

The emerging identification of the state with the nation, and patriotism with nationalism and monarchism, found expression in the 'Great Service of National Thanksgiving' at St Paul's in 1797. This victory parade and service, to give thanks for naval victories, was to a considerable extent the King's idea and it foreshadowed future national celebrations by including in the ranks of the parade ordinary sailors and marines. Nelson's state funeral was another instance of national pride and sorrow which honoured patriotism via elaborate ceremony, although it is significant that George III rather disapproved of such 'national marks of gratitude' being given to one who was not royal. The peace and victory celebrations of July and August 1814 were more becomingly royal, with the Prince Regent as a gilded host amidst his fellow allied sovereigns. Such magnificent state celebrations were far from being a British tradition and were inspired by emulation of the great public ceremonies of republican and Napoleonic France, but Britain could focus them upon the monarchy and draw upon and reinterpret older monarchical traditions. On St George's Day, 1805, a splendid installation of Knights of the Garter was held at Windsor Castle with an extravagant expenditure quite without precedent in the recent past. Napoleon had earlier held a ceremony to institute the *Legion d'Honneur*, soon afterwards crowning himself Emperor, and, as one historian has concluded, 'the Garter ceremony of 1805 was a calculated royal, aristocratic and British riposte, intended to parry the pretensions of a mushroom emperor and his *parvenu* state honours system'.[11]

The celebrations for George III's Jubilee in 1809 demonstrate another side of loyalist feeling and point to the genuine affection felt for the King among the middling and ordinary sort of people, in villages and provincial towns as well as the capital. Accounts of these celebrations can be compared with those of Victoria's Jubilees, or of the Silver Jubilees of George V and Queen Elizabeth II. What is striking is not the differences but the similarities between these occasions, which were at the same time celebrating communities and their sovereign, and which revealed sovereigns as the fathers or mothers of their people. The success of George III's Jubilee reflects the support for it of the respectable middle of British society, and the degree to which loyalty to the monarchy had become inseparable from loyalty to the fabric and institutions of society. It is in the parades of militia, the sermons in churches and cathedrals, the founding of schools and charities, and the dinners given to the poor, that we find the essence of the Jubilee – society saluted its better self and its sovereigns simultaneously. An account of a dinner given for the members of the Freeman's Hospital in Newcastle-upon-Tyne may raise anachronistic hackles at its condescension but we should not conclude that its recipients were anything but grateful for their feast, or loyal to their King. They

> dined together on the green before the house on a plentiful supply of beef, plum pudding, ale, wine etc. Each was provided with their own chair, knife and fork, plates, ale and wine glasses. The decent and orderly appearance of sixty venerable old persons, whose hearts were made glad on this joyous occasion, afforded a sublime gratification to a number of visitors and spectators. The whole was conducted by Mr J. Clark, assisted by a number of free burgesses. Before dinner Mr Clark called the attention of the company to the cause of the festivity and adverted to the long life and happy reign of the King etc. Dinner being over, each member, who chose, was furnished with pipes and tobacco, and several appropriate toasts were given and drank with acclamations and applause. The whole concluded by three o'clock, when Mr C. again made a serious and impressive address to the company, relative to their future conduct. Each female was furnished with a royal blue ribbon, and a new white apron, by Mrs Major Anderson. Mary Huntley, aged 102 years, made one of the party at the table.[12]

Nor were the benefits of the Jubilee celebrations transitory, for in keeping with the monarch's wish that every child should be able to read his bible, many Jubilee schools were founded. By the late 1820s, the Newcastle Jubilee Schools provided free education for some 700 pupils.[13]

By what were effectively the last years of George's reign (from 1810 his illness made necessary the Regency under the Prince of Wales), the monarchy was seen to be widely popular and had become the focus of national sentiment. The vicissitudes of fortune during a long war, and the fear of revolutionary and Napoleonic France, revealed the strength of the monarchy and of the social order of which it was the acknowledged head. What was most impressive was its appeal to the solid middle of society, to voluntary and civic organizations in industrial and provincial towns as well as to gentry society in rural Britain. The fall of the Bastille on 14 July 1789 may well have been a memorable day for European radicalism, but when some three weeks later Parson Woodforde, with thousands of others, came to see George III in Lord Digby's park at Sherborne, it was that day, 4 August, which he prefixed in his diary as '*Dies Mirabilis*', for he had seen his King.[14]

2 George IV and William IV
The Nadir of Popularity?

The reigns of George IV and William IV are often portrayed as marking the lowest ebb in the popularity of the British monarchy. These monarchs have been criticized almost as much by historians as they were caricatured by contemporary cartoonists and satirists. Philip Ziegler has remarked that George IV was 'the most detested man in his kingdom'. J.H. Plumb has gone further and asserted that 'From 1812 to 1837 the Royal Family was held in almost universal contempt', while recently David Cannadine has stated that 'The lives, loves and morals of George III's children were such as to make them arguably the most unloved royal generation in English history'; and John Cannon has concluded that, with this generation, 'the reputation of the Hanoverian royal family reached its nadir'.[1]

Why this almost unanimous disapprobation? Other kings before and after George IV have had mistresses, have lived opulently and extravagantly and have indulged with gusto in food and drink, although few have kept such a modest court as William IV. Most generations have, too, seen some odd, unattractive or unintelligent royal brothers. Often the seven sons of George III have been lumped together as the 'wicked uncles'. Certainly they all shared a partiality for mistresses, liquor and horses. But these tastes were general among a large section of the aristocracy and European royalty of their day, and were not the peculiar peccadilloes of the royal brothers. The Duke of York was an earnest but unsuccessful soldier and a sturdy conservative in politics, while the Duke of Kent, Queen Victoria's father, though also a soldier and a martinet, embraced radical convictions, probably to spite his brother George who could not stand him. The Duke of Cumberland, who became King of Hanover, was a brave soldier and an extreme conservative, he was the most forceful and able of the brothers, but to a good proportion of the population was evil incarnate, being widely, though wrongly, thought to have murdered his valet and fathered a child on his sister. The Dukes of Sussex and Cambridge were quieter types, the one a bookish liberal and the other a career soldier. The Duke of Clarence was almost a parody of the bluff sailor but amiable, without pretensions and not very bright. His reign as William IV is seen as an awkward pause between George's death and Victoria's succession: the reign that nearly everyone but the historian forgets. George, Prince of Wales, Regent and then King, shone above his brothers, not merely because of the position primogeniture gave him but because of his looks, charm and intelligence, though not his common sense.

One important common denominator among the royal brothers was that they were all perpetually hard up and dependent upon the public purse. It is rather unfortunate to be given first place in a society and to find oneself less rich and less independent than a host of aristocrats and wealthy commoners. Here we come back to George III's parsimony. Having wilfully denied himself a decent Civil List, he proceeded to condemn his sons to

'The Vices', a cartoon depicting the vices of the Royal Family as they are personified in George III and Charlotte (Avarice), the Prince of Wales (Drunkenness), the Duke of York (Gambling) and the Duke of Clarence, seen here with his mistress, the actress Mrs Jordan (Debauchery).

a state of splendid bankruptcy – splendid because they could always get loans, and bankrupt because of the compound interest incurred on them.

It was not so much the extravagance *per se* of the royal Dukes that made their expenditure and debts such bones of contention (they were by no means all extravagant as compared with some great landowners) but the fact that they were forced repeatedly to appeal to Parliament for funds. It must be emphasized that George was the worst provided for of any Prince of Wales in the eighteenth century, and his allowance was quite inadequate to maintain the necessary state of his position, never mind his luxurious lifestyle and delight in building and collecting works of art. Thus, the financial difficulties of George and his brothers were an embarrassment to themselves, their friends and supporters and an obvious target for attack by satirists, cartoonists and their political enemies.

At a time when the number of newspapers and broadsheets was increasing rapidly and when the country boasted a number of brilliant cartoonists, both George and William were mercilessly caricatured. Gillray and Cruikshank continually emphasized George's vanity, extravagance and perennial penchant for older women, while William's pear-shaped head and the large bastard progeny he sired with Mrs Jordan, and brought with him and Queen Adelaide to Windsor on becoming King, made him an easily recognisable and vulnerable target.

'A Voluptuary under the Horrors of Digestion', Gillray, 2 July 1792. This cartoon of the Prince of Wales lingering over a meal at Carlton House can be compared with Gillray's depiction of the frugality of George III and Queen Charlotte.

It is difficult to establish just how important the lampooning of the sexual adventures of the Royal Family were or how damaging to the monarchy. It may well be that the more sedate late nineteenth century exaggerated just how shocked contemporaries of George and William were by their public 'private lives'. How shocked, after all, was public opinion in the 1970s by disclosures about Princess Margaret's relationship with Roddy Llewellyn, or in the 1980s by news of Prince Andrew's liaison with Koo Stark? Amused, yes, prurient, perhaps, but shocked? Surely not. Yet a more strait-laced, post-Aids, society may well look back and magnify the impact of such affairs.

George did, however, reign at a time when a long-term shift in manners and morals was occurring, and although much historical writing exaggerates both the completeness and the speed of that shift, it is undeniable that he was unsuited to the moral earnestness and high seriousness that was becoming influential in the 1820s. J.H. Plumb has argued: 'Had both his nature and his time permitted him to graft middle-class virtues on to his sense of theatre he would have become the pattern of modern monarchy. He was born too soon...'[2] It is difficult to conceive of George with 'middle class virtues' and, rather than being 'born too soon', it would be truer to say that he ascended the throne too late.

It is one of the hazards of the royal profession that an heir apparent may spend a long time awaiting his inheritance and that, in that time, he is unlikely to gain much experience of the business of government. British monarchs have tended to be neither kind nor wise in the treatment of their heirs, they have wished them to be responsible but denied them responsibilities. It is, perhaps, in the nature of monarchy that rulers should be reluctant to give their heirs duties which amount to a share of power and position, for to do so diminishes their own majesty and is a reminder of their inevitable demise. The venom and hatred that characterized the relations between the first two Georges and their eldest sons were exceptional, but irritation, exasperation and a certain jealousy seem to have been the normal reactions of sovereigns to heirs apparent into recent times and no monarch has permitted his or her heir to undertake duties of any real substance. Having given his son a strict but ambitious education, George III declined to appoint him to any position of power and influence. Nor was the Prince of Wales allowed to follow the military paths permitted to his brothers. So, a prince possessing considerable erudition, wit and taste, but with little self-discipline, was denied the duties and responsibilities which could have given direction to his life. It is little wonder that he concentrated upon pleasure nor that, in the traditional manner of Princes of Wales, he took up with the political opposition.

George confidently expected the Regency, if not the Crown, in 1788, when he was in his mid-twenties, but the recovery of his father from illness prevented him from becoming Regent until the final onset of that same illness in 1811. All things being equal, young and old monarchs tend to be more popular figures than do the middle-aged. A handsome, though prematurely portly, young man would have taken first place in 1788, a stout and florid middle-aged gentleman became Regent in 1811, while an obese, breathless and gouty figure became King in 1820.

It would be wrong to conclude, however, that George was constantly lampooned solely because of his physical appearance, extravagances and dubious morality: one must also take into consideration the highly volatile political atmosphere of Britain during and after the Napoleonic Wars. Behind the brutal depictions of George IV and William IV, in print and in pictures, was a highly charged political atmosphere. In the early nineteenth century the monarch was not above politics, and during his Regency George demonstrated not only a determination to be the centre of a spectacular display of royal grandeur, but also evinced a considerable tenacity and an ability for getting his own way in political matters. During the war, as Ian Christie has argued, George 'kept intact the royal prerogative of selecting ministers, and obtained what he wanted: a ministry committed to outright prosecution of the war and prepared to avoid raising the troublesome issues of Catholic Emancipation or parliamentary reform'.[3]

In many ways these years were the height of George's popularity. He presided in 1814 over magnificent victory celebrations and over a nation rejoicing in its strength; he had an heir, Princess Charlotte, while his embarrassing wife made the years of victory sweeter by taking herself off abroad. But these halcyon days were not to last. The death of Princess Charlotte in 1817 was a severe blow to George and to the nation. It inspired the Dukes of Clarence and Kent to marry in the hope of providing an heir to the throne, in which Kent's marriage proved succesful with the birth of the future Queen Victoria.

The stampede at Carlton House. After the grand fête with which he inaugurated his Regency, George opened his house to the public for three days. This Rowlandson cartoon shows a crowd tumbling down a staircase on a day when some 30,000 people tried to get in and several women were stripped nearly naked in the stampede.

George had made many political enemies. He was the natural target for radicals and proto-revolutionaries but he had also incurred the hostility of the Whigs who had supported him while he was Prince of Wales, but from whom he had turned on becoming Regent. The post-war years brought more than enough problems and hardships and, inevitably, George and his ministers were criticized and attacked, to such an extent that Peel expressed his concern that if the Royal Family showed too many signs of weakness '…it will be the match to fire the gunpowder'.[4] His fears were exaggerated but when, on becoming King, George determined to divorce Queen Caroline, he provided an ideal opportunity for Whigs and radicals to combine and concentrate their fire on the King and his administration. As a result the Queen Caroline affair turned into an extraordinary and long-running melodrama during 1820 and 1821, a scandal of gigantic proportions which

'The Morning after Marriage – or – A scene on the Continent', Gillray, 5 April 1788. The Prince of Wales and Mrs Fitzherbert had in fact been married three years earlier in 1785.

dwarfs all subsequent royal scandals. Combining elements of politics, morality and street theatre its progress was followed avidly by the nation.

Despite his secret marriage to Mrs Fitzherbert, George had married Princess Caroline of Brunswick in 1795. The motive was economic necessity, his father having flatly refused to increase his annual allowance unless he made a suitable marriage. Unfortunately, it was never a happy marriage. Nine months after the wedding, and immediately after the birth of their daughter Charlotte, Caroline went to live in Blackheath and never again resided in the same house with George. She then adopted a way of life that gave rise to perpetual rumour and scandal. In 1814 she left Britain for the Continent and, once abroad, many scandalous stories circulated concerning her lascivious behaviour and her supposed numerous paramours. George, eager for a divorce, instigated the 'Delicate Investigation' in 1806 and the 'Milan Commission' which considered her activities whilst abroad. Successive governments had, however, been reluctant to institute divorce proceedings, aware that there was a public sympathy for Caroline, that the political opposition would champion her, and that George himself was not in the strongest position to protest moral outrage. But when, on becoming King, George ordered that her name should not be mentioned in prayers for the Royal Family, it became clear that he did not intend Caroline to be crowned Queen. Caroline refused to be cast aside, returned to England, and immediately became a rallying point for

During the Queen Caroline affair many vitriolic articles, cartoons and poems were published attacking George IV, though this one seems to have little sympathy for either party.

diverse political groups and a heroine amongst the lower orders. Wherever she went her reception was rapturous. 'In terms of coverage in the newspapers, radical agitation and popular involvement' it has been called the 'most impressive display of public opinion in the capital since the days of Wilkes'.[5] Emotions were heightened when the Government, in its attempt to deprive Caroline of her title, introduced a Bill of Pains and Penalties into the House of Lords. The evidence presented and published during the reading of the Bill was enough to satisfy the most salacious of readers. At the same time Charles Greville recorded in his diary, 'No other subject is ever talked of… If you meet a man in the street, he immediately asks you "Have you heard anything new about the Queen"… I never remember any question which so exclusively occupied everybody's attention and so completely absorbed men's thoughts'.[6]

In one sense, the Caroline agitation testifies to the strength of monarchism at this period. For although the demonstrators gave expression to discontent with King and government, they did so by supporting an alternative member of the Royal Family. Whigs and radicals may have taken up Caroline's cause for their own particular and diverse ends, and leading radicals may have been simply trying to use Caroline in an attempt to discredit the monarchy, but the mass of Caroline's supporters were, at least for the time being, for the Queen, thereby expressing a somewhat unorthodox monarchism. To the Whigs and radicals she was a political pawn, but to the crowds who cheered her she was a temporary heroine. The reasons for her popularity with the public were interconnected. George was seen as having transgressed the rules which popular culture saw as determining relations between the sexes; this being the case, it was delightful to parade moral superiority to the highest in the land; and it was possible to turn the whole affair into street theatre. When the Bill was dropped, much to George's annoyance, because its majority in the Lords on the third reading had only been nine and it was now clear that it would meet with little success in the Commons, carnival took over. Revels in London were, in Creevey's words, 'beyond everything'. All the main and even 'the most obscure and most quiet streets' were illuminated.[7]

Nevertheless, Lord Eldon's conviction that the agitation would 'die away like all other nine days' wonders'[8] proved to be correct. Despite the many thousands who turned out to line the streets on 29 November when Caroline attended a thanksgiving ceremony at St Paul's, where the psalm chosen was 'Deliver me, O Jehovah from the evil man: Preserve me from the violent man', her victory was a hollow one. She had never, in truth, been a serious figure; fate had, as Max Beerbohm has put it, written her 'a most tremendous tragedy and she played it in tights'.[9] Once the Bill of Pains and Penalties had been dropped, the unity of the opposition crumbled. The Whigs, having achieved their aim of embarrassing the King and his government, now distanced themselves from Caroline, and when in January 1821 an attempt was made in the Commons to have her name put back in the liturgy, it was heavily defeated. Caroline further weakened her position and alienated support when she accepted a pension of £50,000 per annum from the government.

With the political pressure eased, George, actively abetted by the Prime Minister, Lord Liverpool, embarked on a programme of rehabilitation. It was an astute programme which took into account the popular appeal of lavish and spectacular ceremonies. Of course, George was by no means the first king to appreciate the importance to the monarchy of grand ceremonial occasions, but very often in the past these spectacular events had been confined to London. His father, in his sixty years' reign, had not travelled far from the capital, so George's tours to Ireland, Hanover and, in particular, Scotland heralded an important and successful development in strengthening the social influence of the monarchy. It was a move which was to be copied and expanded by all future monarchs.

The first great ceremony was, however, George's coronation. For most people it was the first coronation within living memory and the government, aware of the need to recapture the support of the London crowds, decided upon a lavish spectacle, for which purpose they obtained from Parliament the enormous sum of nearly a quarter of a million pounds. It was an event which admirably suited George's sense of theatre and he spent much time in supervising the arrangements and the making of the gorgeous coronation robes. Caroline's attempt not to be excluded from the event was a humiliating failure. Supported by what Croker described as a 'thin and shabby mob',[10] she was prevented from entering the Abbey and forced to make an ignominious departure.

Within a fortnight after the coronation, George had embarked at Portsmouth for his state visit to Ireland, the first such visit since the time of Richard II. Upon receiving news of the serious indisposition of Caroline, it was thought prudent to delay the crossing to Ireland and land at Holyhead. On 8 August came the news of her death. Surprised and yet relieved, George gave orders for the royal yacht to set sail again for Ireland. During the journey he celebrated the loss of his wife with large doses of whisky, so that by the time of the landing he and his companions were, according to one report, 'in the last stages of

The Prince of Pleasure

An engraving by Robert Havell & Son of George IV's entry into Dublin on 17 August 1821. This visit, like his visit to Edinburgh the following year, was a tremendous success.

intoxication'.[11] Nevertheless, George managed to carry off all his duties that day with grace and dignity and, in turn, was enthusiastically received by the Irish. Indeed, wherever he went during the three weeks of his stay, he attracted large crowds, some of whom no doubt wished to cheer a king who had taken the trouble to visit Ireland while others still believed in the almost supernatural status of the monarch. The Duke of Melrose, writing from Dublin Castle on 31 August, noted that large crowds 'have pressed upon the King to see and to touch him, a little inconveniently, and mixed perhaps with some superstition, as if some good would happen to them in some way or other, from having touched the King or his clothes'.[12]

Another incident also reveals the almost godlike status in which the king was held by some. One eyewitness reverentially reported that on leaving Dublin and embarking on the royal barge, George 'appeared to be walking on water'. An Irishwoman, desperate to plead with the King for the life of her son who had been sentenced to death for robbery, attempted to follow him and almost drowned. On learning of this incident, George extended his popularity by pardoning her son.[13]

The visit was both a political and a personal success for George. Yet within eight days of his return he was off again on another state visit, this time to Hanover. But it was the following state visit, to Scotland, the third within the space of a year, which proved to be his greatest triumph.

The Scottish tour was originally planned to take place in 1823 but Lord Liverpool, fully aware of the success of the visit to Ireland, urged George to advance his plans and go in the summer of 1822. Elaborate arrangements were made on the part of the Scots, the

British government and the King himself, to make this a great occasion. Sir Walter Scott, who had attended George's coronation and had marvelled at its sumptuousness and sense of history, supervised arrangements for the pageantry and processionals in Scotland. The Tory ministers also attempted to ensure there would be a sense of occasion in London. Lord Eldon wrote on 10 August: 'The King is to be off this morning and there is every preparation to make his embarkation and voyage down the river one of the finest exhibitions ever seen upon the surface of old Father Thames…'[14] Finally, George spent much time in preparing for the visit, mainly in ensuring that his wardrobe was appropriate and ornate. His bill from the firm of George Hunter of Tokenhouse Yard and Edinburgh came to over £1,300.[15]

Compared to ceremonial occasions today, the organization of the visit appears rudimentary, if not inefficient. Perhaps the fault lay largely with George himself, but very few people were aware of when the King was actually setting off for Scotland. Many newspapers announced that his departure would take place on Thursday the 8th. Large crowds flocked to Greenwich on that day and the following day, only to be disappointed. It was not until the afternoon of the 10th that the long-suffering crowds, together with the Lord Mayor of London, who had organized a flotilla of barges to accompany the royal yacht down the Thames, witnessed the departure of the King.

Similar uncertainties existed in Scotland. On 18 July the Lord Provost of Edinburgh received a letter stating that the King would be expected to reach Edinburgh 'on or about the 10th of August'.[16] Not only did this not give the Scots much time to prepare for the visit but once again the large crowds, which assembled on the tenth, were to be disappointed. The King finally arrived in Edinburgh on the fifteenth. In most other respects great care was taken over the visit. Although travelling in the royal yacht from London to Edinburgh may have been quicker and more comfortable than journeying by land, it was also more politically acceptable, for no one wanted to be reminded of the Duke of Cumberland's excursion over the Border in 1746. Shortly after George had disembarked he was greeted by Sir Walter Scott, who presented him with a silver cross of St Andrew which George pledged himself to wear, hence giving visual proof that he was King of Scotland. The same reasoning lay behind his wearing of the Royal Stuart tartan (the effect of which was somewhat spoilt by the flesh coloured tights he wore under his kilt) at the grand levee held at Holyrood. By doing so, George was hoping to show the reconciliation between the houses of Stuart and Brunswick.

Everywhere George went he was greeted by vast crowds. One reporter estimated that on 15 August 300,000 people crowded into Edinburgh to see him. As this accounted for about half the population of Scotland, it was certainly an exaggeration. Nevertheless, there was no doubting the interest and enthusiasm that the visit aroused. Once again, as in Ireland, it became clear that to some Scots the concept of kingship, if not one of divinity, was one of a very special nature. Even the Lord Provost in his speech of welcome referred to his 'Majesty's sacred person'. But George's behaviour was much more that of the secular king, and shortly after this speech one writer noted that, as he passed a house in Picardy Place, the balcony of which 'was occupied by a number of beautiful females… The King seemed delighted with the loyal demonstrations of this fair bevy, to whom he most graciously bowed'.[17]

'A Fishing Party'. A Heath cartoon of 27 June 1827. The fat and gouty King, living in seclusion at Windsor, is having to be helped to the river by his mistree Lady Conyngham and Sir William Knighton. The implication is that the King is a puppet in their hands.

Overall, the two-week visit was an immense success but it proved also a very heavy strain on the sixty-year-old King. During the next few months his health declined rapidly. Madame de Lieven in January 1823 stated that she 'found the king changed' and that he had 'aged a great deal in the last three months'.[18] His breathlessness and gout had worsened and his swollen feet and legs made it difficult for him to walk. The pain was considerable but to George, who had always taken vast pride in his looks and dress, what was equally distressing was his worsening physical appearance.

There was no doubt that the cruel caricatures of George as an increasingly fat and swollen parasite lavishing his money on himself and his mistresses hurt his pride, and his growing reaction from 1823 onwards was to hide that fat and swollen body away from the public gaze. He spent much of his time in seclusion at Windsor and when he did travel to London, he did so very often in secrecy. His visits to Brighton became rare and although he did make public appearances at Ascot, the theatre, the opening of Parliament and the funeral of the Duke of York in January 1827, the occasions when he was seen in public became fewer and fewer. By 1827 his legs and feet were so swollen that he was unable to walk up steps, and increasingly he was having to make use of a wheelchair.

When George finally died in June 1830 few really mourned his loss. He had been out of the public eye too long for his death to instil any genuine grief. In addition, as Greville pointed out, the opposition press continued to rake up 'all his vices, follies and misdeeds' which, he had to admit, 'were numerous and glaring enough'.[19] Certainly, George possessed vices in plenty but it is unfortunate that a concentration on them has obscured many of his actions, which reveal a man genuinely concerned with the role of the monarchy in society. George not only subscribed to various literary and scientific funds but he also gave personal encouragement to a number of individual scientists, artists and writers. One of these was Sir Walter Scott whom he invited to Windsor in 1826. Scott recorded in his diary how kind and courteous the King was to him, 'in many respects the model of a British monarch'. His only concern was George's 'sort of reserve, which creeps on him daily and prevents him going to places of public resort'.[20]

George possessed extravagant tastes but he often spent wisely. He collected magnificent examples of eighteenth-century French furniture and his art collection contained a superb array of seventeenth-century Dutch paintings of which he was justly proud, and which he was quite ready to loan for exhibition – as he declared, it was not formed 'for my own pleasure alone but to gratify the public taste'.[21] In addition, George was instrumental in urging the government to buy collections of paintings which then formed the nucleus of the National Gallery.

The vast sums of money which George expended on buildings incurred the wrath of many of his contemporaries. The money spent on the Pavilion at Brighton and the Royal Lodge at Windsor, and the virtual reconstruction of Buckingham Palace and Windsor Castle, amounted to many millions of pounds. This interest in royal homes, his influence upon fashion and dress and his patronage of the arts and sciences, were aspects of royal behaviour which were to be developed and built upon by subsequent monarchs. But perhaps the most important development during George's reign was his appreciation of ceremony and spectacle. He realized the potential of presenting the pageantry and splendour of monarchy to a wider audience than 'Society'. He saw that ceremony could be great theatre and that such theatre need not be confined to London. He did not simply restore the glitter and magnificence of the Stuart monarchy, but linked an older notion of the grandeur of monarchy fascinating an awestruck populace with the new delight of involving a knowing populace in royal show. More than most of his contemporaries, he realized not only that the grandeur and opulence of royalty are inseparable from its function, but that they become more important as the function becomes more titular and the man in the street more sophisticated. He was the first monarch to view his role with an eye influenced by the Romantic Movement and to see the traditional ceremonies of monarchy as events which could be embellished by looting the past, real and imaginary, to provide backdrops for present majesty. It was a development which royal successors have paid heed to and adapted for their own particular purposes.

These important contributions have been obscured by two factors. The first is that George's domestic circumstances marked an abrupt departure from the cosy marital felicity of George III. Such felicity, although it escaped every alternate monarch from Victoria to George VI, has been seen, rightly, as an important aspect of the appeal of modern monarchy. The second was the controversial political position of the Crown throughout George's Regency and reign; years in which, although the power of the Crown showed some decline, ministers remained very much the King's ministers, and when the issues raised by the Test and Corporations Acts and Catholic Emancipation brought the Crown back to the forefront of politics.

Finally, after the success of the Coronation and the Royal tours, George, in the discomfort and shame of his infirmity and corpulence, slowly but steadily retired from public view. It was this, just as with Victoria after the death of Albert, which contributed most towards his unpopularity. He had re-established the public splendour of the monarchy, only to then hide from it. As Huish wrote soon after George's death, 'The Royal Family of England… has long been regarded by the country as a species of public property, in which the humblest subject of the land claims a deep and lively interest'.[22] In these circumstances retirement from public life is the ultimate sin.

It was a sin which the new King was determined not to commit. In fact, William tried very hard to be everything that his brother had not been. Right from the start informality and accessibility were the order of the day. J.H. Plumb wrote aptly of George IV that whatever his faults he had style.[23] It would be equally pertinent to state that whatever his virtues William IV possessed no style. Whereas George loved ceremony and ostentation, was a patron of the arts and loved racing, William preferred informality, was in most things economical, had no tastes in art and detested racing. But in one important sense William was much more a man of his time than George. By refusing to follow many of the traditional aristocratic pursuits, William's lifestyle was much more in accord with that growing and influential section of the population, the middle class. As Hobhouse remarked, of both William and Queen Adelaide, 'the worthy couple are like wealthy bourgeois… All this is worth recording only in contrast with our late Asiatic monarch'.[24]

William, at first, tried hard to be a popular king. He immediately allowed the public once again to use the terraces and drives in the Windsor Home Park, a privilege which had been suspended by George in his concern that the people should not see him hobbling or being wheeled about. William also appeared in London frequently and, at first, on his own. Greville recorded in July 1830 that William went 'on a ramble about the Streets all alone too'. He proceeded along St James's Street where, 'he was soon followed by a mob making an uproar, and when he got near White's a whore came up and kissed him'.[25] The new King also instituted economies. George's French chefs were dismissed, his German band was replaced by a British one, the staff at Windsor was reduced in number, the expensive gas installations were removed, and most of the Royal Lodge at Windsor was pulled down. In addition the royal stud was reduced by half, the animals in George's menagerie were sent to the London Zoo, only two of five Royal yachts were retained and many of George's art treasures were handed over the nation.

William also resolved not to have a coronation ceremony, which he regarded as extravagant, outdated and a form of mere antiquarianism. He suggested that instead he should merely take an oath before the assembled members of the two Houses of Parliament. But he did not get his way. His ministers were wise enough to realize that crowds love bread and circuses and that society and the London crowd must not be deprived of such an occasion. In the end, a compromise was reached and the 'Half Crownation', so called because only £30,000 was spent on it compared with the £240,000 ten years earlier, took place on 8 September 1831. Despite the economies, the young Macaulay at least was extremely impressed by the occasion, although it was apparent to him that some parts of the ceremony were ill-organized. He wrote of

> …the magnificence of yesterday. No pageant can be conceived more splendid… At eleven the guns fired, the organ struck up, and the procession

entered. I never saw so magnificent a scene. All down the vista of gloomy arches there was one blaze of scarlet and gold... The Queen behaved admirably, with wonderful grace and dignity. The King very awkwardly... The ceremony was much too long, and some parts of it were carelessly performed. The Archbishop mumbled. The Bishop of London preached well enough indeed, but not so effectively as the occasion required; and, above all, the bearing of the King made the foolish parts of the ritual appear monstrously ridiculous, and deprived many of the better parts of their proper effect. The moment of the crowning was extremely fine.[26]

There is no doubt that in the first months of the reign the prestige of the monarchy was raised, but it is difficult to determine whether this was effected by William's own efforts, or whether he was swept to popularity by the political circumstances of the time. For William came to the throne just at the time that the ultra-conservative Charles X was overthrown in France and when demands for parliamentary reform were being firmly expressed throughout all parts of Britain. The general election called on the death of George resulted in a swing away from the Tories; when the Tory government was defeated in the Commons in November 1830, William could do little other than send for Lord Grey to form a Whig administration which, it was popularly thought, would introduce measures for the reform of Parliament. So, although William was by no means a reformer he was, almost inescapably, associated with the political changes that had taken place over the previous six months. His political popularity rose further in April 1831 when, after a defeat in the Commons on a clause in the Reform Bill, Lord Grey persuaded William to grant a dissolution of Parliament and call new elections. By so doing William 'had safeguarded the Bill by dissolving, and it was mistakenly inferred from this that he must be an ardent reformer. The electors were exhorted, in a play on his name, to 'vote for the two Bills'... Within a few days of the dissolution the Theatre Royal, Drury Lane, was advertising the inclusion of 'God Save the King' in the programme and putting on 'Alfred the Great, or the Patriot King', with Macready in the main part'.[27]

In fact, William was highly embarrassed by this image of himself as a popular hero and a supporter of parliamentary reform. Neither he nor Queen Adelaide were happy with the proposed legislation. When this became apparent in the following year, their popularity in the country plummeted. William's refusal in April 1832 to create fifty new peers in order to defeat the Tory majority in the House of Lords, followed by his acceptance of the resignation of the Whig ministry, cast him, in the eyes of many, as the villain of the piece. There were protests and demonstrations throughout the country and now, far from being able to walk about the streets on his own, he was booed, hissed and had stones thrown at him as he passed in his carriage. Adelaide was even more unpopular as it was supposed, with some justice, that she was entirely against reform and it was assumed, perhaps too readily, that she had great influence over the king in political matters.

It is noticeable, however, that once the Reform Bill was passed and the political temperature dropped, so William was restored to some sort of popular favour, although it never again reached the heights of the early days of his reign. When he died, in 1837, the *Spectator* summed him up as 'A weak, ignorant, common-place sort of person...

During the early stages of the Reform Bill, William was believed to be in favour of parliamentary reform. In this Doyle cartoon he is shown searching for an honest politician.

DIOGENES IN SEARCH OF AN HONEST MAN.

sufficiently conceited and strongwilled'. Yet the paper conceded that he was, 'to the last a popular sovereign'.[28] Compared with his predecessor, William's life style was monotonously mundane. He and Adelaide lived a quiet life of domesticity, dividing their time between London, Brighton and Windsor, and in many ways they appeared like and appealed to the respectable middle classes of the country. Adelaide's philanthropy further strengthened the role of the monarchy as leading and encouraging society's charitable impulses. At the same time, by shunning ceremonials and glittering royal occasions and refusing to be a leader of fashion, William parted company with the traditional followers of the court circle.

In these respects William trod a path which was followed by Victoria and Albert later in the century. But William never entirely escaped criticism from the groups to whom he was trying to appeal. His life with Mrs Jordan, and their ten offspring, were never forgotten by writers or cartoonists and William's loyalty to these children did him no good whatsoever. The *Morning Chronicle* reflected a considerable body of critical feeling when it commented, 'Can anything be more indecent than the entry of a sovereign into his capital, with one bastard riding before him, and another by the side of his carriage?'[29] These criticisms were intensified during times of political turmoil, and William was not a king, as was seen during the passing of the Reform Bill, to allow his political preferences to remain beneath the surface. This was a period when the political power of the monarchy was in decline, but while William could do little to stop it, he certainly did not actively assist in this decline. The popularity and influence of the monarchy were still interwoven with the political circumstances of the time and this was a factor which disappeared only later during Victoria's reign.

The throne that Queen Victoria inherited from William was, nevertheless, secure enough. Bluff honesty, goodwill and a distaste for last ditches had enabled the monarchy, like the aristocracy, to bend to change but to retain much of substance. Philip Ziegler's valedictory comment on William that others, including his brothers, 'would have done worse',[30] is more than faint praise.

3 Victoria with Albert
The Appeal to the Middle Classes

The drama of an inexperienced girl of eighteen succeeding to one of the greatest thrones in Europe is one which has captured the imagination of generations of Britons. From the time that David Wilkie depicted Victoria at her first Council meeting as an innocent young girl in a virginal white gown (she would, of course, have been wearing a black mourning dress) there has been a host of gloriously romantic portraits of the young Queen, showing a vulnerable but beautiful and self-possessed young woman at the time of her accession. This vision of the young Victoria has been retained and further romanticized in the twentieth century, through the medium of the cinema, and in many of the numerous books about Victoria. In her biography, *Victoria R.I.*, Lady Longford relates how the Lord Chamberlain and the Archbishop of Canterbury arrived at Kensington Palace in the early hours of the morning of the 20 June 1837 to inform Victoria of the death of William IV. She was awoken by her mother the Duchess of Kent, who then led her to the room where the two men were waiting.

> Together they descended the awkward flight hand in hand for the last time…
> A cotton dressing-gown covered Victoria's nightdress and her long, light hair streamed down her back. At the door of her sitting-room she parted from her mother and Lehzen, entering the apartment, as she noted in her Journal, *'alone'*. She saw her visitors fall on their knees; she heard Lord Conyngham's first explanatory phrases. When he reached the word 'Queen', she shot out her hand for him to kiss even more swiftly than she had given 'Uncle King' her 'little paw'. It was not merely the efficient performance of a well-rehearsed act. Victoria would have stretched out both hands if etiquette had allowed. After so much travail she was grasping the glorious future.[1]

Although many of those near to her and those who attended her first Council meeting were impressed by Victoria's demeanour and self-possession, the young Queen by no means immediately captured the hearts of the nation. In succeeding two monarchs whose reigns had been short-lived and not exactly glorious, Victoria's was not an easy inheritance, and her accession met with a certain amount of apathy. Greville recorded how on 21 June, when she drove to St James's Palace to be formally proclaimed Queen, he was 'surprised to hear so little shouting, and to see so few hats off as She went by'. Later when, surrounded by her ministers, she appeared at a window of the palace, she 'curtsied repeatedly to the people, who did not, however, hurrah till Lord Lansdowne gave them the signal from the window'.[2]

In the next few months, strenuous efforts were made to raise Victoria's popularity. Receptions were held at which 'the people who really counted in English political, social, and commercial life' met and kissed the Queen's hand.[3] There was also a succession of

'Victoria at her first Council Meeting', by David Wilkie. One of the first of many romanticized portraits of Victoria as Queen. She is depicted here in a virginal white gown, whereas, of course, she really wore a mourning gown.

public ceremonies and processions which brought Victoria to the notice of her wider public. The highlight was the Coronation in June 1838 when Londoners, not to be denied their spectacle, turned out in their thousands to line the streets. As with William's Coronation the organization of both the ceremony and the procession was less than professional. Of the procession, the Earl of Malmesbury observed that it was chaotic because no orders had been issued to the police 'to make carriages keep in line, and there was in consequence a good deal of confusion, coachmen cutting in etc'. He also found that the crowd, although they were in a good humour, 'behaved very quietly'. His conclusion was that although it was a magnificent show 'we had to thank the foreign ambassadors for the great part of this splendour, as without them the procession would have been very little more brilliant than when the Queen goes down to the House of Lords to open Parliament'.[4]

Victoria herself was pleased with the Coronation and with her reception by the crowd, but she was aware that she and her family were not universally popular. A proposal soon after her accession to raise her mother's annuity, while passed, was not well received by Parliament. Although the Civil List was passed without amendment her Prime Minister, Lord Melbourne, was forced to admit that it had been a difficult task and had been achieved largely because of the leader of the opposition's goodwill and his own ability to keep several of the discontented Tories in check.

The major reason for the disaffection of the Tories was of Victoria's own making. A strong-willed, emotional and at times inflexible young woman, Victoria felt no need to hide her preference for the Whig party in general and the Prime Minister, Lord Melbourne, in particular. Some Tories regarded Victoria as a 'Prisoner' of the Whigs and the ultra-Tory Duke of Newcastle was convinced she was 'entirely in the hands of vile ministers'.[5] But Victoria was by no means a helpless and unwilling victim. In a position at last to shake off the stultifying and claustrophobic attentions of her mother, the Duchess of Kent, and her adviser, the despised Sir John Conroy, Victoria went outside the immediate court circle and eagerly sought the advice and guidance of the urbane and handsome Lord Melbourne, who at this time was in his late fifties. Her seemingly complete reliance upon Melbourne and her obvious delight when he was in her presence soon earned her the nicknames 'Mrs Melbourne' and 'Queen of the Whigs'. Her utter dependence upon Melbourne and the emotional intensity which she invested in this relationship was manifested in May 1839 when, after only just scraping a majority on a major division in the Commons, the Whig Cabinet decided that there was no other alternative but to resign. When Melbourne broke the news to Victoria she reacted hysterically and wrote in her journal, 'All ALL my happiness gone!… ' On the following morning she wrote to Melbourne,

> The Queen thinks Lord Melbourne may possibly wish to know how she is this morning; the Queen is somewhat calmer; she was in a wretched state till nine o'clock last night, when she tried to occupy herself and try to think less gloomily of this dreadful change… on waking this morning, all – all that had happened in one short eventful day came most forcibly to her mind, and brought back her grief; the Queen, however, feels better now; but she couldn't touch a morsel of food last night, nor can she this morning.[6]

Such partisanship inevitably earned Victoria resentment and criticism in court and political circles, as well as in the country at large. Part of her behaviour can be put down to youthful inexperience, but only in the sense that she exhibited a naive intensity in her devotion towards the Whigs. Victoria, like her predecessors, believed she had a political role to play and this was reflected in many of her actions during these early years of her reign.

Two incidents in particular, the Bedchamber Crisis and the Lady Flora Hastings affair, illustrate both Victoria's inexperience and her active involvement in political affairs. Both events left her open to criticism and abuse both in the press and amongst her political opponents, and perhaps the surprising fact was not the extent of the unpopularity that Victoria drew upon herself, but that she escaped comparatively lightly despite her indiscretions and partisanship.

The first event, the Bedchamber Crisis, occurred immediately after the resignation of the Whig Cabinet in May 1839. Victoria, now forced to call upon Sir Robert Peel to form a Tory administration, refused point blank, when requested by Peel, to make a few changes among the personnel of her Ladies of the Bedchamber, all of whom came from Whig families. There is no doubt that Victoria hoped that her intransigence on this matter would help foil Peel's effort to form a Ministry. She admitted as much in a letter she wrote to Melbourne during the crisis: 'I think you would have been pleased to see my composure and great firmness… Keep yourself in readiness, for you may soon be wanted'.[7]

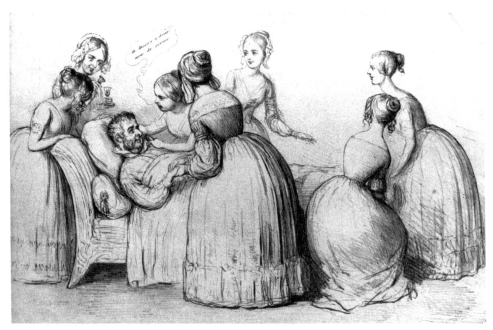

'Resuscitation', a Doyle cartoon dated 24 June 1839. Printed at the time of the Bedchamber Crisis, it shows Victoria and her ladies reviving Lord Melbourne in the hope that he will soon be well enough to return to office.

Victoria interpreted Peel's request for change among the Ladies of the Bedchamber as 'an attack upon my power'[8] On the other hand, Greville declared that 'It is a high trial of our institutions when the caprice of a girl of nineteen can overturn a great Ministerial combination'.[9] In the end Peel declined to form a Ministry and Victoria's beloved Melbourne was reinstated as Prime Minister. Victoria was ecstatic at her victory but it was won at considerable expense. The monarchy was heavily criticized by sections of parliament, the press and the public. No future monarch dared to enter into a similar battle and no future administration was prevented from taking office because of the particular predilections of the monarch.

If the Bedchamber crisis brought her unpopularity among large sections of the population, however, this unpopularity was exacerbated by the scandal involving Lady Flora Hastings, which started in early 1839, continued throughout the Bedchamber crisis and was not laid to rest until the autumn of that year.

The Flora Hastings affair was the sort of juicy scandal beloved by both press and public and rumours, accusations and counter-accusations concerning it made popular reading in the press during the spring and summer of 1839. Lady Flora Hastings, who came from a Tory family, was a lady-in-waiting to Victoria's mother, the Duchess of Kent. Although she was unmarried it appeared to Victoria early in 1839 that Lady Flora was pregnant and, it was whispered, by Sir John Conroy, previously the Duchess of Kent's private secretary, a man whom Victoria hated and whom she had dismissed shortly after becoming Queen. The rumours concerning Flora's pregnancy grew and Victoria insisted that she should be medically examined. The resultant diagnosis was that, far from being pregnant, the unfortunate Lady Flora was suffering from an enlarged liver. The Hastings family, angered at the indignities heaped upon her and at the reluctant apology secured from Victoria, satisfied all sorts of press speculation by allowing their correspondence with the Court on this matter to be published by the Tory newspaper, the *Morning Post*. Victoria's reputation suffered, and the reception she received at Ascot that year was far from favourable. But worse was to come. Lady Flora's health continued to decline and she died on the morning of 5 July. The autopsy revealed a tumour on the liver, although her supporters claimed that she had died of a broken heart as a result of the ignominy and ill-treatment she had received. The funeral drew a crowd of 5,000 and the repentant Victoria sent a carriage to the funeral which had to be guarded by police for fear of attack. The pros and cons of the scandal continued to be aired throughout the summer, the *Morning Post* leading the way with a number of virulent attacks on Victoria.

During the course of the scandal Greville gave as his opinion that it contained the potential to arouse 'just the sort of feeling which prevailed at the time of Queen Caroline'.[10] The affair had all the right ingredients: rumours of illicit sex, a wronged woman and a monarch who was proved wrong. But although these events never brought about anything like the disturbances witnessed in 1820, Greville's remark should not be discounted entirely. One major reason why the outcry against Victoria was not so vociferous and vicious as it had been against George IV was that the nature of the opposition to the monarchy was different. George had been confronted by an opposition at least part of which was fundamentally opposed to monarchism, and a large section of the remainder had little compunction about embarrassing the King. But in 1839 it was the Tories who were aggrieved. Their parliamentary leaders, Peel and Wellington, both of whom implicitly believed that their prime duty as politicians was to serve the Crown, could never encourage direct attacks upon the monarch. Perhaps, if Lady Flora Hastings had come from a Whig family and if the Bedchamber crisis had been over a monarch refusing to replace her Tory ladies in-waiting with Whig ones, then the outcry from radicals and disaffected Whigs would have been on a much larger scale than that actually created by the Tories. In a year which saw the first of the major Chartist petitions, the threat to social stability and the resulting problems presented to Crown and Parliament could then have been considerable. The Tories, of course, did attempt to make political capital out of the two events, but they were hamstrung by their own political convictions. As the Duke of Wellington confided to Greville, Victoria 'deserves the severest reprehension, but the castigation She merits cannot be administered without impairing the authority, the dignity, the sanctity of the Crown she wears, and it is necessary to spare the individual for the sake of the institution'.[11]

Another reason why the outcry against Victoria was comparatively muted, so Michael Wynn Jones argues, was that by 1839 there were no longer any great satirical cartoonists around to attack her. 'The great surge of inspiration set rolling in the 1780s had exhausted itself'.[12] But satirists do not exist in a vacuum, and by 1839, although there were still deep divisions within the country and working-class discontent was being channelled into the new Chartist movement, much of the alienation felt by the urban commercial and industrial middle classes had been eliminated by the parliamentary legislation of 1828 to

1832. In fact, it was to this rapidly growing section of the population that Victoria had most appeal, especially after her marriage to Prince Albert in 1840.

At first sight the marriage appeared far from propitious. Although most politicians wanted Victoria to marry and to produce an heir to the throne, so that there was no possible chance, in case of her premature death, of her being succeeded by her almost universally hated uncle, the King of Hanover, there was a general reluctance to see Victoria married to a foreign prince. Victoria's cousin, Prince Albert of Saxe-Coburg-Gotha, had for a number of years been marked out as a possible husband for her. But both Lord Melbourne and Victoria had doubts about the advisability of such a marriage. Victoria, because she did not wish to endanger her new-found freedom, and Melbourne because he was well aware of the British dislike of foreigners. He, along with other politicians, feared that marriage to a foreign prince who might then become a powerful influence over her would endanger that popular quality of 'Britishness' that George III had brought to the throne. However, in October 1839 Albert, together with his brother, visited Britain and Victoria was immediately bowled over by his good looks. Within five days of his arrival in the country, Victoria had proposed to Albert and the marriage was arranged.

While Victoria fell madly in love with Albert, politicians, press and public were much less enamoured of this prince from a remote, near-bankrupt, German state. The Tories, still angry over the Bedchamber Crisis, successfully joined with other discontents in the Commons to reduce the proposed annual allowance to Albert of £50,000 (the same sum given to the wives of George II and George III) to £30,000. Distrust of foreigners was also manifested in the concern expressed in Parliament that Albert, like some of his Coburg relatives, might have strong leanings towards the Papacy. Consequently, the Commons insisted on the word 'Protestant' being added to the word 'Prince' in the official declaration of Victoria's marriage. There was also disagreement concerning Albert's precedence in the royal hierarchy. Victoria wanted Albert to be made King Consort, but this suggestion was anathema to many and in the end it was decided that the matter of Albert's precedence should be shelved until after the marriage. In fact, the first step towards solving the problem occurred in 1840 after Victoria, who was four months pregnant, survived an assassination attempt whilst out driving in a coach with Albert. As so often happens when an entrenched institution is seriously threatened, the existing apathy or even discontent towards it evaporates and is replaced by demonstrations of enthusiasm and loyalty. Such was the case on this occasion. Stories of Victoria and Albert's courage during and after the incident abounded and they were cheered heartily wherever they went. The attempt on Victoria's life also raised, in an urgent form, the question of who should act as Regent if Victoria died leaving a minor as heir to the throne. Parliament acted quickly, and a Regency Bill making Albert sole Regent was passed without any opposition.

Once established as Victoria's husband, Albert came to be more and more respected, but he by no means captured completely the confidence of all sections of the population. His Germanic seriousness and aloofness did not endear him to the working people, and much of 'Society' continued to look down upon this prince from a socially inferior German royal family. What alienated the aristocracy even more was that Albert showed very little interest in their company. He never joined any of the fashionable men's clubs; he disliked small talk and gossip, and his manner all too clearly showed that he regarded many of them as empty-

A satirical comment on Prince Albert's Teutonic arrogance in seeking to improve that most aristocratic of British industries, farming. From Punch *magazine, October 1844.*

PRINCE ALBERT THE BRITISH FARMER.

" Prince Albert has turned his attention to the promotion of agriculture, and if you have seen, as most probably you have, an account of the sale of Prince Albert's Stock, and the prices they fetched, I have not the slightest doubt you will give one cheer more to PRINCE ALBERT AS A BRITISH FARMER."—*Sir Robert Peel's Speech at Tamworth, October 2, 1843.*

headed, if not dissolute. As Albert's influence over Victoria grew, so she too drifted away from their company. In her early years as Queen, Victoria had delighted in London, court ceremonies, balls and late-night parties. Albert clearly preferred early nights, the comparative peace of Windsor and later Osborne and Balmoral, to London and the social round. For many visitors, evenings spent with the Royal Family at Windsor or elsewhere seemed dull, and the entertainment provided was not nearly as varied as in many other English country houses. What was worse for those in court circles was that court ceremonial, which had been relaxed during the reign of William IV, was now, partly through Albert's influence, made rigidly formal. Strict regard was paid to court dress and etiquette and the rules applied to behaviour in the company of Victoria and Albert were precise and stringent.

In the last resort, however, it was his essentially Germanic qualities which estranged him from so many of the aristocracy. Although Victoria was hardly less German than Albert, he was clearly German 'by birth, education and temperament'.[13] This could be seen in his bearing, his speech (he spoke German to Victoria for most of the time), his clothing (he observed on one occasion that 'no tailor in England can make a coat'), and in his attitude to sport. Although Albert enjoyed riding to hounds, he disappointed his fellow huntsmen with his German hunting outfit, by 'not sitting on horseback in the English manner'[14] and by his

SPORT! or, A BATTUE MADE EASY.

Prince Albert's decidedly un-British enthusiasm for efficiency, even in the sporting field, led contemporaries to make fun of his delight in the Battue, *a highly organized shoot in which great quantities of game were driven towards stationary guns.*

insistence on stopping for a hot lunch. He also greatly enjoyed a *Battue*, which by the aristocracy was regarded as both unsportsmanlike and decidedly un-British.

Albert was a serious man who was more at ease in the company of intellectuals and industrialists than with *bon viveurs* and society wits. He took a deep and diligent interest in the arts, sciences and education; the architect Robert Rawlinson contended that he had such ability that 'To an architect he could talk as an architect, to an engineer as an engineer, to a painter as a painter, to a sculptor as a sculptor, to a chemist as a chemist, and so through all the branches of Engineering, Architecture, Arts and Science'.[15] These wide-ranging interests and new ideas were not always appreciated. Many dons in the traditional institution of the University of Cambridge seriously challenged his election to the Chancellorship in 1847, and although Albert was victorious, the ultra-conservativism of the dons was such that his role was restricted to that of a figurehead rather than an innovator.

The Prince was much more successful in his role as President of the Royal Society for the Encouragement of Arts, Manufactures and Commerce. In this capacity he promoted the industrial design exhibitions of 1847, 1848 and 1849, and he and Henry Cole were the most hard-working and committed members of the Society in organizing the Great Exhibition of 1851. Albert intended the Exhibition to be a monument to British craftsmanship and scientific progress, and to the ideals of free competition, free trade and individual endeavour.

In 1850, Punch *satirized Albert's difficulty in raising funds for the Great Exhibition. Whatever Albert turned his hand to, the satirists found occasion to disparage.*

THE INDUSTRIOUS BOY.
"Please to Remember the Exposition."

Also, in his own words, it was to give 'a true test and a living picture of the point of development at which the whole of mankind has arrived...'[16] In one sense, what Albert was doing was voicing the hopes and beliefs of a wide assortment of people involved in the professions, industry and commerce, who were benefiting materially from the enormous advances which were making Britain the foremost industrial and commercial power in Europe. Not only was Albert in accord with middle class beliefs in progress, free competition and capitalism, but he and Victoria also led a private life which was very much in line with middle class values and expectations. While previous monarchs had been patrons of the arts and sciences, few, and certainly not their immediate predecessors, could claim the moral respectability which was justly attributed to Victoria and Albert. In this respect, their private lives contrasted sharply with those of George IV and William IV and, at a time when society was increasingly concerned with the virtues of home and family, they and their nine children appeared the epitome of a respectable happy family.

There is no doubt that their social habits were much more akin to those of the affluent sections of the middle classes than to the aristocracy. Their conception of an enjoyable evening was a family one, singing duets together, partaking in 'round' games and playing with the children. In her journal Victoria, time and again, records her intense enjoyment at being alone with Albert and the children. In 1844 she confided to her uncle, King Leopold of the Belgians: 'God knows *how willingly* I would *always* live with my beloved Albert and our children in the quiet and retirement of private life, and not be the constant object of observation and newspaper articles'.[17] Some overnight guests were certainly bored by the seemingly dull evenings spent by the royal couple, but most commented on the family's obvious contentment. The Earl of Malmesbury, who was an early visitor to Balmoral, wrote in his diary in 1852 that although his 'room was so small that I was obliged to write my despatches on my bed and to keep the window constantly open to admit the necessary quantity of air', the evenings were spent in a most informal way. He and Albert played 'billiards every evening, the Queen and the Duchess [of Kent] being constantly obliged to get up from their chairs to be out of the way of the cues. Nothing could be more cheerful and evidently perfectly happy than the Queen and Prince, or more kind to everybody around them'.[18]

Theirs was a private family life which increasingly became common knowledge as more and more family journals and magazines came on to the market in the 1840s and 1850s. In particular, the growth of the pictorial press, (the *Illustrated London News* started publication in 1842), played a large part in conveying to their middle class readers an idealized version of royal family life. Invariably, whenever the family travelled to Windsor or Osborne or Balmoral, these publications printed sketches of them, of the houses and even some of the furnishings in the houses. Inevitably, these furnishings were scrutinized, admired and very often copied. In 1848, the year of revolutions in Europe, while many royal thrones were under threat, the *Illustrated London News* in December printed a drawing of Victoria, Albert and their children in front of their Christmas tree. This illustration, depicting happy family life, not only gave a massive boost to the purchase of trees at Christmas time and established the tree as an integral part of the British Christmas festival, but it also reflected the stability of the British monarchy compared to some of its continental counterparts.

During these years, Victoria above all enjoyed her time spent with Albert at Osborne and Balmoral. The comparative inaccessibility of both places meant that privacy was easily secured. But, unlike George IV in his later years and Victoria herself after the death of Albert, the royal couple did not fall into the trap of making it clear that privacy took a higher priority than national duty. Despite her regular pregnancies throughout the 1840s, Victoria not only travelled around Britain but also visited the Continent on a number of occasions. In 1842 Victoria and Albert went to Scotland for the first time and, in the following year, Victoria became the first British monarch to visit France since Henry VIII. Two years later the royal couple travelled to Germany and visited Albert's birthplace, and in 1849, in an attempt to heal some of the wounds incurred during the Great Famine, they visited Ireland.

At first, just as in the days of George IV, the tours were ill-organized. On the visit to Scotland in 1842 there was no official announcement of when the royal party would board their yacht at Woolwich, and consequently there were very few people present to cheer them on their way. Also, although very large crowds assembled in Edinburgh on 31 August to line the route of the procession, the royal fleet was late in arriving. In fact, the voyage had been an extremely rough one and Victoria and Albert, who were not good sailors at the best of times, were badly seasick. Understandably, when the yacht arrived early on the morning of 1 September, Victoria insisted on landing at the earliest opportunity. The Royal party then made its way into Edinburgh 'at an earlier hour than was anticipated' and 'the City was taken entirely by surprise'.[19] There were comparatively

This illustration, printed in the Illustrated London News *on 23 December 1848, did much to popularize both the Christmas tree and family Christmases.*

Victoria and Albert in Ireland, Illustrated London News, *18 August 1849. The visit was made in an attempt to improve Anglo-Irish relations after the Great Famine.*

few people lining the route and when the Lord Provost, Magistrates and members of the City Council hurried to the gates in order to perform the civic ceremony of handing Victoria the keys of the City, they were too late; the royal procession had already passed through.

One major problem bedevilling the smooth organization of the tour was the impossibility of predicting accurately when a sailing boat leaving London would reach Scotland. On this occasion it took three and a half days, and on the return journey Victoria and Albert forsook their yacht, the *Royal George*, for the *Trident*, a steam boat belonging to the General Steam Navigation Company. This journey was accomplished in two days. Not surprisingly, after this experience, in the following year they had their own steam yacht built and launched.

The development of the railway system in the 1840s made it much easier to arrange successful royal tours throughout the country. It was from this time on, and for the first time ever, that the monarchy became not merely a London-based institution, but one which was able to transfer some of the spectacle and display associated with it to the provincial cities and towns of Britain. At the same time, the organization of the tours was improved. In 1851, when Victoria and Albert were persuaded to break the journey on their return to Windsor from Scotland and make a two-hour tour of Lancaster, the town was first visited by the Earl of Carlisle who met the town dignitaries and inspected all the parts of the town where it was proposed the royal party should visit. Only after he was satisfied did the tour go ahead. If the official chronicler of the event is to be believed, it was a great

Her Majesty passing a Triumphal Arch on Her trip to Scotland on the Great Northern Railway.

The rapid development of the railways facilitated countrywide royal visits. The railways also enabled the Queen to spend much of the summer at Balmoral.

success. 'Admiration of our gracious sovereign was the theme of every tongue. From the highest to the lowest one feeling of devoted attachment prevailed... Much of this good feeling was, we are persuaded, owing to Her Majesty's personal demeanour. The Plainness of Her Majesty's costume and the other absence of display charmed every heart'.[20]

Significantly, although Albert was a prominent figure in this royal visit, it was Victoria who received nearly all the praise. For to many Englishmen Albert, despite all his virtues and endeavours, remained essentially a foreigner. Yet it was Albert who had done so much to secure Victoria's popularity. It was he who was the prime mover in setting a high moral tone at court and in developing the image of a respectable home-loving royal family.

Yet arguably his greatest achievement was to realign the role of the monarchy in political affairs. His influence over Victoria was such that he was able to disentangle her from her too close association with Lord Melbourne and the Whig party. From then onwards the Crown, while exerting influence, especially in the realm of foreign affairs, could not be accused of patronage towards one particular political party. It was a path which paid dividends, at least in respect of ensuring the popularity of Victoria, if not Albert himself. Even during the height of the Irish crisis at the end of 1845, The *Examiner* newspaper asserted that, despite 'the pranks and bunglings of the last three weeks, there is one part which... has been played most faultlessly – that of a Constitutional Sovereign'.[21] Victoria, and Albert in particular, were assiduous in working through the numerous despatch boxes sent to the Monarch by her ministers. They commented on documents, and proffered advice and information when they thought it necessary. At times their advice was warmly welcomed. Lord Malmesbury, when he became Foreign Secretary in Lord Derby's administration in 1852, wrote in his diary, 'I owe much to the Queen and the Prince, who, in the kindest and most gracious manner, give me a great deal of private information of which I could know nothing as to foreign, especially German, Courts'.[22] On other occasions, however, and with different personalities, notably Lord Palmerston, their 'interference' was not welcomed.

Albert's growing influence over Victoria, after their marriage in 1840, brought many changes. In December 1845, when Lord Lansdowne and Lord John Russell had an audience at Windsor, they compared their reception with their previous visit when they had last held office, in 1841. Then the Queen received her ministers alone, now Albert was present and both of them always referred to 'We'. Greville concluded that Albert had 'become so identified with her that they are one person, and as he likes and she dislikes business, it is obvious that while she has the title he is really discharging the functions of the Sovereign. He is King to all intents and purposes'.[23] For some of the time this statement came close to the truth, especially at times when Victoria was forced to withdraw from public life as a result of her many pregnancies.

Later, in the 1850s, a decade which saw six different administrations, all of which had small parliamentary majorities, Lord John Russell was to remark of Albert that he 'was an informal but potent member of all cabinets'.[24] It was largely the confused political climate and the comparative weakness of the administrations that brought this about. Yet Albert's prominence led to fears that he was becoming too powerful. It was claimed by the popular and radical press, not totally unjustly, that a major reason for Palmerston's dismissal as Foreign Secretary in 1851 was Albert's dislike of his policies and of his habit of neglecting to send drafts of his despatches to Victoria before transmitting them to British embassies abroad. Again, in 1853, when Palmerston, now Home Secretary, proffered his resignation, it was asserted that he had been placed in this position by Albert. At various times throughout the 1850s all sorts of rumours, some containing an element of truth, others so far-fetched as to be laughable, but all casting Albert in an unfavourable light, circulated in the popular press. At one time it was suggested that Albert was a Prussian agent and, later, on the eve of the outbreak of the Crimean War, it was claimed that he was a Russian spy and that he had been arrested for treason and sent to the Tower. This last rumour achieved such currency that crowds of Londoners flocked to the Tower in order to 'see his Royal Highness go in'.[25] Victoria was distraught at these attacks on her beloved Albert and, although counselled by Uncle Leopold to ignore them, for 'Abuse is somewhat the *staff of life in England'*,[26] she was terribly aggrieved at what she thought was the sheer ungratefulness of the British public.

Nevertheless, the antipathy to Albert drew away any potential criticisms of Victoria herself and, with him as whipping boy, her popularity remained high. This was no mean achievement in a period when most European royal families came under severe attack and, if not deposed from power, certainly could not claim the loyalty and support that Victoria received. In this respect, Victoria's indebtedness to Albert was great, and the importance of his role was emphasized in the years following his untimely death in 1861.

4 Victoria without Albert
Imperialism and Grandeur for a Widow in Weeds

'The things of this world are of no interest to the Queen, beyond the satisfaction she must experience if Peace is maintained, and the country is in prosperity: for *her* thoughts are *fixed above*… The eternal future is her only comfort'.[1]

Queen Victoria in a letter to Lord John Russell.

The loss of Albert came as an overwhelming blow to Victoria who, during her twenty-two years of married life, had become increasingly dependent on the Prince, not only in state and political affairs, where he had advised her and even drafted her letters, but also in personal, family and social matters. The country, too, was shocked at the news of his death on 14 December 1861. The *Times* sold more papers than ever before in its history, 89,000, on the day it published the news of Albert's death. Partly out of respect for Albert and partly through compassion for Victoria, the nation mourned. A traveller passing through London on 16 December found the 'shops in Shoreditch were shut up – all blinds down – up to Buckingham Palace'. On the day of Albert's funeral, Lord Broughton described London as like 'a city struck by the Plague', and in churches throughout the country large congregations solemnly listened to funeral sermons. It was a sombre time. 'No one wishes each other "A *merry* Xmas" this year' wrote Mrs Gaskell and, years later, Flora Thompson recalled being told that 'when the Prince Consort died every lady in the land had gone into mourning'.[2]

Victoria donned her widow's weeds, a style of dress she was to retain for the rest of her life, and observed strict mourning. She was anxious that her family should do the same and curtly informed Earl Granville in June 1862, when asked whether she would permit the Prince of Wales to present prizes at the International Exhibition being held in London, that she had 'laid it down, as a principle, founded on deep feeling, that none of her sons and daughters should take part, during this year of grief, in any public ceremony'.[3]

After 1862, members of the Royal Family once again went out into society and, in the case of the Prince of Wales, at least in Victoria's eyes, with an unseemly zest and enthusiasm. Victoria, however, preferred the seclusion of Osborne and Balmoral and surrounded herself with mementoes, paintings, photographs and busts of her loved one. She continued mourning Albert for the rest of her life and, even in an age where mourning was an integral element in respectable social behaviour, her manifestations of grief were undoubtedly excessive. There is a story that twenty years after Albert's death, when Disraeli himself lay dying, it was proposed that Victoria visit him. Disraeli declined the offer on the grounds that 'She would only ask me to take a message to Albert'.[4]

Despite her mourning and her deep and undoubted grief, Victoria did not retire completely from her royal duties. Although she missed Albert's sound advice, she continued to work her way through the numerous despatch boxes and still insisted on being kept informed of state affairs. Just before leaving for a visit to Coburg in the autumn of 1863, and remembering past occasions, she wrote to Lord Palmerston reminding him again of 'her desire that *no step* is taken in foreign affairs *without* her *previous sanction* being obtained'.[5] Her seclusion may have helped to give the impression to Walter Bagehot, among others, that the power of the Crown had declined more dramatically than it had. Victoria insisted firmly upon her prerogatives and, without Albert's restraining influence, was to return to her old path of political partisanship for the rest of her reign, championing Disraeli and Salisbury and detesting Gladstone. As John Cannon has perceptively observed, the importance of Bagehot's view of the working of constitutional monarchy is not that it was a true picture at the time at which he wrote but that, because it was widely believed to be accurate and future sovereigns were raised on Bagehot, it was to become true.[6]

The essential difference between pre- and post-1861 was that Victoria now was only very rarely prepared to give up her seclusion in favour of state duties, and ministers who needed to consult her were very often forced to make the long and uncomfortable journey to Balmoral before they could obtain an audience. In addition, her dislike of London and, more significantly, her dread of appearing in public now that she no longer had her revered royal escort, meant that the number of court ceremonials and state occasions was severely restricted. Victoria employed all manner of excuses to avoid taking part in public ceremonies. A woman of robust health, she claimed that she was physically and mentally incapable of undergoing the rigours and stresses of such occasions. In 1865, when it was suggested that she re-open Parliament, her reaction verged on the hysterical and she urged her doctors to inform those concerned that her nerves and constitution were not sufficiently strong for such an ordeal. It was not, she explained to Earl Russell, that she wanted 'to shut herself up from her loyal people' for she would 'seize any occasion which might afford to appear amongst them (painful as it even is now) providing she could do so without the fatigue or exertion of any *State* ceremony entailing full dress etc'. In the following year she was finally prevailed upon to perform this duty, although she compared it to 'an execution' and complained '*very bitterly*' about 'the want of feeling of those who *ask* the Queen to go to open Parliament'.[7] Even then Victoria insisted that she retain her widow's weeds and enter Parliament only through the Peers' entrance, and that the Speech be read for her by the Lord Chancellor.

Only on six occasions between 1861 and 1886 did Victoria agree to open Parliament, and it is significant that these occasions invariably coincided with a need for her to request Parliament to vote annuities to members of her family.

It was Victoria's reluctance to participate in state ceremonials that led one modern historian to write that the period 1861 to 1881 was 'the nadir of royal grandeur and ceremonial presence', and forced Walter Bagehot, in 1874, to conclude that 'the Queen has done almost as much to injure the popularity of the monarchy by her long retirement from public life as the most unworthy of her predecessors did by his profligacy and frivolity'.[8] But Bagehot's primary concern at the lack of spectacle, taken together with the immediacy of the events he was describing, prevented him from appreciating just how strong the social influence of the monarchy had grown since the early years of her reign and how entrenched and popular the institution had become in the past two decades.

Victoria's reluctance to participate in public life is highlighted by this Punch *cartoon of 1865 in which Britannia pleads for her to give up her seclusion. 'Tis time! Descend: Be Stone no more!' (The Winter's Tale, Act I, Scene iii).*

QUEEN HERMIONE.

There were criticisms of Victoria in the media, most of which concerned her protracted seclusion, her avoidance of London and her marked preference for her Scottish servants, but compared with the intensity and bitterness of the attacks directed towards George IV forty years earlier, they were lightweight and even deferential in tone. What was frustrating for Victoria's advisers was that if she had been a little less selfish and had been prepared to forget Albert for a short while, she would have immediately silenced her critics. Victoria, however, was a singularly stubborn woman and no amount of pleading would change her mind. On one occasion even the Prince of Wales entreated his mother:

> If you sometimes even came to London from Windsor – say for luncheon – and then drove for an hour in the Park (where there is no noise) and then returned to Windsor, the people would be overjoyed – beyond measure. It is all very well for Alix and me to drive in the Park- it does not have the same effect as when you do it; and I say thank God that is the case. We live in radical times, and the more the *People see the Sovereign* the better it is for the *People* and the *Country*.[9]

Victoria remained obstinate and, as her unenforced seclusion continued, so criticisms increased. Much of the gossip centred around John Brown, originally a stable hand on the

The famous cartoon by Matt Morgan, 'A Brown Study', which shows John Brown standing between an empty throne and the British lion.

staff at Balmoral, whose devoted loyalty and strength, and probably even his rough manner, attracted Victoria. She came to rely on him increasingly and in 1865 he was promoted to the post of the 'Queen's Highland Servant'. As Victoria told her uncle, '[I] have *now* appointed that excellent Highland servant of mine to attend me ALWAYS and everywhere out of doors… and it is a *real* comfort, for he is *so devoted to me – so simple, so intelligent, so unlike* an ordinary servant…'.[10] Brown now attended the Queen not only at Balmoral but on public visits and during her stays at Osborne and Windsor. In March 1866, when Victoria was persuaded to visit Aldershot and review the troops, the *Morning Post* announced that she was accompanied by 'Ghillie Brown'. During the next few months, all manner of unfounded rumours circulated. Brown, it was claimed, dominated Victoria completely and was, in reality, the power behind the throne. In July, *Punch* published a fictitious Court Circular which centred on Brown's and not the Queen's activities. 'Balmoral, Tuesday. Mr John Brown walked on the Slopes. He subsequently partook of a haggis. In the evening, Mr John Brown was pleased to listen to a bag-pipe'.[11] Later that summer a Swiss newspaper declared that Victoria had secretly married Brown and was pregnant. *Reynolds News* picked up the story and although it was not given much credence, Victoria was given the nickname of 'Mrs Brown'.

In July 1867 the Prime Minister, the Earl of Derby, expressed concern when Victoria let it be known that although agreeing to review the troops in Hyde Park, she intended to be accompanied by John Brown. Derby had received information which suggested that if John Brown did appear on this occasion, there could well be some form of public demonstration and there was a possibility that the Queen's coach would be attacked. When Victoria's equerry finally plucked up courage and suggested to her that Brown should not attend, Victoria reacted as expected. She firmly informed him that 'The Queen will not be dictated to, or made to alter what she has found to answer for her comfort'.[12] The matter was unexpectedly if unfortunately resolved, when on receiving the news of the execution of the Emperor Maximilian in Mexico, the court went into mourning and the review was cancelled.

It is difficult to assess to just what extent there was general public disapprobation directed towards Victoria resulting from her relationship with John Brown. Doubtless the English prejudice against 'foreigners', and particularly those who threatened to become influential with the monarch, played some part, but it is noticeable that newspapers and magazines were unable to maintain public interest in 'John Brown rumours' for any length of time. What is clear is that John Brown was bitterly disliked by most other members of the Royal Family and those politicians and members of the court circle who came into close contact with him. They resented his brusque manner, his privileged position and the degree to which Victoria obviously admired and depended upon him. It was this small but influential section of society, rather than the country at large, who worried about John Brown. Also at times, as in the case of the Hyde Park review in 1867, it is hard to separate direct criticisms of Victoria's behaviour from specific political agitation. Lord Derby's main concern in July 1867 was not so much John Brown's accompanying Victoria, but that the Reform League, dissatisfied with the proposals of the Second Reform Bill, might use the occasion to embarrass both the government and Victoria. As it was, the review was cancelled and the opportunity for a demonstration was lost, but in the following years a number of radical politicians and political groups included in their targets for attack the institution of the monarchy in general, and Victoria's behaviour as Queen in particular. The trade union paper, *The Bee-Hive*, on a number of occasions raised the issue of the sums of money awarded to the Royal Family and how they were spent. In September 1871 a pamphlet entitled 'What Does She Do With It?' appeared and two months later, the radical politician, Sir Charles Dilke, in a speech in Newcastle-upon-Tyne, attacked Victoria for being party to political corruption and failing to perform her duties. He concluded by suggesting that a republic would be a preferable alternative to the monarchy. Dilke's declaration in favour of republicanism was not an isolated incident. Doubtless inspired by recent events in France, republican ideas were circulating in Britain, and by the end of 1871, there were some eighty-four republican clubs established in the country.

Soon after Sir Charles Dilke's sensational speech, the Prince of Wales contracted typhoid fever. His condition deteriorated and for a few days it was feared that the heir to the throne might die. During these critical days Victoria wrote in her journal: 'The feeling shown by the whole nation is quite marvellous and most touching and striking, showing how really sound and truly loyal the people are. Letters and telegrams pour in and no end of recommendations of remedies of the most mad kind'.[13] The *Times* for its part dropped all discussion of world and home events and confined its leaders solely to the subject of the Prince of Wales's health. Throughout the country bulletins concerning the progress of the Prince were eagerly awaited. In the remote parish of Clyro in Radnorshire on 14 December, the tenth anniversary of Prince Albert's death, the Reverend Francis Kilvert wrote in his diary, 'today the Prince is better. Thank God'. Three days later he noted, 'What a blessed happy contrast to the suspense and fear of last Sunday. How thankful we all are'.[14] At the thanksgiving service at St Paul's in February 1872, held to celebrate the Prince of Wales's recovery, it was estimated that well over a million people lined the street from Buckingham Palace to St Paul's in order to cheer the Prince and Victoria.

The public's reactions to the illness of the Prince of Wales and his subsequent recovery have led some historians to conclude that it was crucial in stifling the criticisms of Victoria and the institution of the monarchy. One historian has written in terms of a 'curiously dramatic change of public opinion'; Lady Longford, in her biography of Victoria, declared that 'Typhoid fever, which had just failed to despatch her son, destroyed Dilke's campaign, and dealt republicanism a crippling blow', and Stanley Weintraub concluded that 'republicanism was all but dead'.[15] These are appealingly romantic interpretations but are too simplistic and, by implication, overestimate the extent to which both republicanism and dissatisfaction with Victoria were prevalent.

Despite the various criticisms made by Bagehot, Dilke and others, the monarchy in 1871, even compared with thirty years earlier, was firmly entrenched and deeply respected. In 1841 Parliament had expressed its disapproval of the monarchy by passing an amendment whereby the proposed annuity to Prince Albert was drastically reduced. Now, at a time when Victoria was supposed to be under severe attack, the nearest Parliament came to challenging her was when a minority of fifty-one MPs voted to reduce the proposed income for Prince Arthur from £15,000 to £10,000! Outside Parliament, compared with the 1820s, newspapers and magazines were generally supportive of the monarchy, those that were not had precarious existences. Even the *Tomahawk* magazine, which had produced some of the most biting cartoons in the late 1860s attacking Victoria, and which claimed a circulation of 50,000 with its issue containing the Matt Morgan cartoon 'A Brown Study', had folded by the end of 1870. Also, by 1874 only a handful of republican clubs remained. The roots of republicanism had never been more than fragile and it was very much a minority interest. Again, despite all Dilke's efforts, he found it difficult to sustain his own personal support, let alone convince the public of the monarchy's association with political corruption.

The only criticism of substance levelled against Victoria in the 1860s and 1870s related to her continued seclusion and the lack of state ceremonial. But, in one respect, even this criticism has been over-stressed by commentators and historians. Perhaps they have concentrated overmuch on the fears and concerns expressed by the politicians and people close to Victoria, rather than focusing on the reactions of the public towards Victoria and state events. Her public appearances were limited, but whenever she did visit a town or unveil a statue of Albert, the crowds who turned out to see her were enormous and enthusiastic. As a contemporary writer, T.H.S. Escott, pointed out, although some popular periodicals read by the working classes might be unfavourable to the monarchy, 'Yet when the sovereign appears in public the reception is one of the highest enthusiasm – the very men who a few hours before may have given vent to sentiments positively seditious are

After 1872 the Queen went out in public more frequently, a major factor in restoring her popularity. Here the Illustrated London News *of 2 April 1872 shows her visiting the East End of London.*

borne away on the tide of general feeling, and applaud the pageant to the echo'.[16] When Victoria visited Wolverhampton in 1866 she recorded in her journal her usual feelings of being 'so *alone*, without my beloved husband' but went on to add, 'The enthusiasm was very great... We drove back through... the poorest part of the town... There was not a house that had not got its little decoration, and though we passed through some of the most wretched-looking slums, where the people were all in tatters, and many very Irish-looking, they were most loyal and demonstrative'.[17]

Even criticisms concerning the lack of Court functions have to be treated carefully. There had been many in the Court circle who had been thoroughly discontented with the lack of social life even when Albert had been alive. In any case, after the marriage of the Prince of Wales in 1863, these critics gravitated towards and stayed at Marlborough House. Disraeli called the celebrations after the wedding 'a royal public honeymoon extended over months', and one of Edward's biographers had recorded that the wedding 'began such a season as London had never previously known' and it led to 'a social sovereignty which endured until his death'.[18]

Despite Victoria's insistence on her own continued personal mourning, public spectacle and ceremony were not entirely eliminated. The wedding of the Prince of Wales was a major event and treated as such, as was the arrival in London from Denmark of Princess Alexandra and her family. Met by the Prince of Wales at Gravesend, the party travelled by train to London and then formed a carriage procession which passed through many parts of the capital. Vast crowds assembled to catch a glimpse of the young couple and the scenes were chaotic. The Earl of Malmesbury observed that the streets in the City were blocked 'and if it had not been for the good temper of the people some terrible catastrophe must have occurred. As it was there was great danger opposite the Mansion House, and the Danes were much frightened'. The wedding ceremony at Windsor again proved a great spectacle, although confusion reigned outside and the special train arranged to take the guests back to London was totally inadequate. 'The Duchess of Westminster, who had on half a million's worth of diamonds, could only find place in a thirdclass carriage, and Lady Palmerston was equally unfortunate. Count Lavradio had his diamond star torn off and stolen by the roughs'.[19]

Occasions like this were rare, but certainly not eliminated, during this period. In any case, in the last resort, it was not the aristocracy or the working people who provided the backbone of support for Victoria or the institution of monarchy. It was within the ranks of the middle classes that Victoria found her most enthusiastic supporters, and the rapport built up with them while Albert was alive was intensified and reinforced during these years. Victoria's devotion and mourning for her departed husband was something which was part and parcel of respectable middle class morality and was admired rather than criticized. Her popularity was such that when her book, *Leaves from the Journal of our Life in the Highlands, 1848-61* was published in 1868, 20,000 copies were sold straight away and many other editions soon followed. The rapid, widespread and large sales of this book, together with those of *More Leaves*, published in 1884, clearly reveals that although some critics may have complained about her lack of public appearances, there was a large body of opinion within the country who admired her style of living quietly in the country with her Scottish servants. One reason, it has been claimed, why Victoria was persuaded to publish her *Highland Journal* was that she hoped it would have a salutary effect on the upper classes (those people whom she believed were continually leading the Prince of Wales astray) by presenting them with a picture of the 'good, simple life'.[20] Whether this was the case or not, the book was praised by most reviewers, bought in large quantities by Mudie's circulating library and read avidly by the respectable middle classes. As Mrs M.A. Everett Green wrote, 'In families where moral tone is natural and beautiful, it will be read with deep and sympathetic interest'.[21]

In one sense the success of the book was to the detriment of Victoria and her desire for seclusion. It rekindled the interest in things 'Scottish', and the area around Balmoral became a resort for tourists who came by train and made every effort to catch a glimpse of the Queen, either by attending the local church or by touring the countryside in the hope that they might see her out riding.

The *Highland Journal* recalled to its readers part of Victoria and Albert's life together, but the public really needed no reminder of Albert. Although Victoria may have sought seclusion for longer than her advisers would have liked, the memory of the Prince Consort remained firmly in the limelight and the public in most cities and towns throughout Britain in the 1860s and 1870s could scarcely avoid reading about him, or seeing statues, memorials or other buildings being erected in his honour. The fact was that Albert became more popular after his death than he ever was when alive. Victoria, of

Many of the tributes to Prince Albert were of great practical value to local communities. This is the Albert Memorial Industrial School, Birkenhead.

course, did a great deal to promote his memory. She commissioned the publication of a volume of his addresses and speeches which appeared in 1862, and carefully supervised and scrutinized the biography of Albert which she asked Sir Theodore Martin to write. Victoria was also the moving spirit behind the endeavours to erect a national monument to Albert in London. However, it would be wrong to conclude that it was owing solely to the Queen's efforts that 'the cult of the Prince Consort' developed during this period. Immediately after the news of Albert's death, there was public demand for some sort of reminder of him. Around 70,000 carte-de-visite size photographs were sold: Arthur Munby recorded that it was only after much searching that he was able to find a cheap portrait of Albert, and when he did he gave 'four shillings for what would have cost but eighteen pence a week ago'.[22]

Throughout the country, most of the schemes for memorials to Albert were drawn up and pursued, not by the palace, but by various corporations, institutions and local benefactors. Indeed, the desire of local authorities to erect their own memorials to Albert seriously affected the efforts to raise money for the national memorial in London. Some tributes to Albert were funded by municipal authorities or by private donors, but the majority came about through public subscriptions. By the end of Victoria's reign, there were more statues of the Prince Consort erected throughout Britain and abroad than of any previous dignitary. If towns did not erect statues, they commemorated Albert's name in other ways, very often in new buildings: institutes, colleges, hospitals, almshouses, drinking fountains or clock towers, all of which, they could claim, were of practical use within their own communities.

For occasions such as the unveiling of memorials to Albert, Victoria did agree, although not invariably, to appear in public. It was an aspect of her public duties which was to

*In 1890 Victoria was still
unveiling statues of Albert. On this
occasion it is J.E. Boehm's statue
in Windsor Great Park.*

continue for the rest of her reign. Her first public appearance after the death of the Prince Consort was in Aberdeen on 13 October 1863, when she unveiled a statue of her late husband, although she insisted on this particular occasion that, as the Court was still in deep mourning, there should be no cheering, no bands playing and that houses and buildings should not be gaily decorated. Twenty-seven years later Victoria was unveiling yet another statue, this time in Windsor Great Park.

As early as 1862 Lord Torrington had gloomily predicted that if all the plans for memorials to Albert went ahead, 'every town in England will have some miserable work of art'.[23] Certainly, there were many who criticized the aesthetic qualities of some of the structures erected during these years, but very often the driving force behind public subscriptions was the local leaders of industry and commerce, men who were not necessarily well-versed in the relative merits of architecture and design, but who had most admired Albert while he was alive and who concurred wholeheartedly with his views on progress, the application of science to industry, free trade and laissez-faire. It was these industrialists and entrepreneurs who wanted local memorials erected: in honour of Albert, out of sympathy for Victoria, because it reflected well upon themselves, and because the statue, clock tower or whatever would stand as a conspicuous demonstration of the wealth and affluence of the town, something which had come about, so they believed, through an adherence to the policies and outlook which they and Albert held in common.

It was also, in many cases, these men and their wives who composed the membership of the planning committees set up in most towns and villages throughout Britain to celebrate Victoria's Golden Jubilee. As well as sumptuous celebrations in the capital involving Victoria herself, it was hoped that local festivities in honour of her fifty years' reign would exceed anything in living memory. For despite the contemporary problems of poverty, unemployment and industrial discontent, there seemed to be plenty of reasons to rejoice. By 1887, only a minority of people in the country could remember any other British monarch, and no other British monarch had been the head of an Empire which covered about one-fifth of the world's land surface. In addition, as the head of a large royal family, many members of which had married into other European royal families, Victoria was now regarded not merely as the head of a great empire but also as the matriarch of Europe. Whereas, in the earlier part of her reign, under the guidance of Albert, Victoria had largely withdrawn from involvement in politics, now she was regarded as being *above* politics. As one of her biographers has stated, by 1887 Victoria was 'As much myth as monarch… she could do little wrong except in the eyes of the extremists, to whom few paid any attention'.[24]

The evidence of countrywide Golden Jubilee celebrations does not ineluctably lead to the conclusion that the entire population was wholeheartedly in favour of Victoria or of monarchy as an institution. It has been argued that such occasions are primarily ones organized and manipulated by the dominant élite in order to promote their own particular system of values, and it does not follow that these values are automatically accepted by all sections of the population. The opportunity for working men and women to snatch an extra day's holiday, for example, could be to them more of a consideration than celebrating Victoria's fifty years as Queen. Also, the wide coverage of such celebrations could obscure the fact that many people were apathetic or even hostile to the Jubilee. But while Hammerton and Cannadine, in their examination of Cambridge at the time of the Diamond Jubilee in 1897, concede that the organization, and therefore the content of the celebrations, were dominated (as one might expect) by the local élite, they were forced to the conclusion that in Cambridge at least 'the majority of the population did want to celebrate'.[25] There is no reason to suspect that this conclusion would be widely different for other parts of the country at this time or, indeed, ten years earlier at the time of the Golden Jubilee.

Around the time of this first Jubilee a new sense of working-class involvement with the Queen and the Royal Family becomes apparent. Instead of a distant loyalty to a rather abstract figure there is a new personal interest, not just in the Queen herself or even the Queen and the Prince of Wales, but in the family as a whole and in the personalities of its members. Newspapers and magazines began to cater for the interest in royalty they detected in the increasingly literate working classes, and to bring news and photographs and illustrations of royalty into working-class homes in country villages and provincial towns. As with the middle classes, this absorption in the private lives of royalty appears to have been particularly marked among women and to have reflected the combined appeal of majesty and domesticity, glamour and common family situations, to a female audience.

Flora Thompson described vividly the preparations for the Golden Jubilee that took place in her Oxfordshire village. Weeks before the actual celebrations the women of the village contributed towards the national Women's Jubilee gift fund, a fund which eventually amounted to £75,000. The village women gave 1d each, 'And when the time

Jubilee Dinner for old people, Sutton Coldfield, 24 June 1887. Celebration and charitable concern for the poor came together in this dinner.

came for the collection to be made they had all of them their pennies ready. Bright new ones in most cases for, although they knew the coins were to be converted into a piece of plate before reaching Her Majesty, they felt that only new money was worthy of the occasion'.

Flora Thompson's village combined with two others to celebrate the event. 'Nothing like it had ever been known before' and the programme of the festivities – a special tea, sports, dancing and fireworks in the park belonging to a local magnate – must have been replicated in hundreds of towns and villages throughout the country.

> As the time drew nearer, the Queen and her Jubilee became the chief topic of conversation. The tradesmen gave lovely coloured portraits of her in her crown and garter ribbon on their almanacks, most of which were framed at home and hung up in the cottages. Jam could be bought in glass jars adorned with her profile in hobnails and inscribed '1837 to 1887. Victoria the Good', and, underneath, the national catchword of the moment 'Peace and Plenty'.[26]

Victoria herself was apprehensive about taking part in the celebrations, especially the planned procession to Westminster Abbey for the Thanksgiving Service, and she steadfastly refused to wear her crown and robes. Nevertheless, she was impressed and

The Illustrated London News *reproduced this painting by G. Amato, depicting the splendour of Victoria's Diamond Jubilee as she arrived to attend the Thanksgiving Service at St Paul's Cathedral.*

excited by the events and afterwards issued a statement from Windsor Castle thanking the nation for the kind reception she had received. Once again, Albert figured large in her thoughts. 'The enthusiastic reception I met with… has touched Me deeply. It has shown that the labour and anxiety of fifty long years, twenty-two of which I spent in unclouded happiness shared and cheered by My beloved Husband, while an equal number were full of sorrows and trials, borne without His sheltering arm and wise help, have been appreciated by My People'.[27]

Not only did Flora Thompson partake of the festivities in her village but she, like many others, was now able to experience something of the grand pageantry of the London celebrations. For with the developments in printing and illustration techniques, cheap Jubilee editions of newspapers and magazines were sold and were now within the price range of large sections ofthe population. This was even more the case with the Diamond Jubilee in 1897, when some national newspapers were selling at $\frac{1}{2}$d a copy. By this time, Victoria had reigned longer than any other British monarch in history. The achievement of this milestone naturally enhanced her personal popularity, but the fact that it came at a time of such industrial growth and imperial expansion transformed her into a revered symbol. The authorities in cities, towns and villages determined to surpass even the events of 1887. This was the culmination of Victorian spectacle and grandeur. Colonial prime ministers and troops came over to London to take part in the ceremonies and a quarter of a million pounds was spent in the capital on street decorations. No expense was spared in order to fête and honour Victoria. The celebrations were a great success. Bagehot's advice, that 'It is better to spend a million in dazzling when you wish to dazzle, than three-quarters of a million in trying to dazzle and yet not dazzling',[28] was well and truly heeded.

One innovation at the Thanksgiving Procession in 1897 was to be, for later royal occasions, of prime importance. A film was made of the procession arriving at the steps of St Paul's. Victoria agreed that this new process was amazing but she found the pictures 'a little hazy and too rapid'.[29] No one in 1897 could appreciate just how influential this new media would be during the next century in presenting the monarchy to the public.

5 Edward VII

The Importance of not being George

The portly shadow of George IV loomed over Edward VII for most of his life. His parents, his tutors, the clergy and much of the press all saw the former king as the very antithesis of an ideal modern monarch, and every slip of Prince Albert Edward's from the path of moral rectitude and high seriousness was accompanied by solemn warnings that he was in danger of coming to resemble his 'wicked' great uncle. 'Even the body of average respectable opinion felt', so E.F. Benson recorded, 'the gloomiest anticipation of the probable effects of his accession and wondered whether the days of George IV would return'.[1] This apprehension is in some respects easy to understand, for as Prince of Wales, Edward had been involved in a number of well publicized scandals. He had been subpoenaed to appear in two court cases, the Mordaunt divorce suit in 1870 and the Tranby Croft case in 1891, and his keen liking for and close involvement with members of the opposite sex had also not escaped the notice of the media. Perhaps it is not surprising, therefore, that at the time of his accession even the respectable and deferential *Times* newspaper wrote: 'We shall not pretend that there is nothing in his long career, which those who respect and admire him could not wish otherwise'.[2]

Fears that Albert Edward had the making of another George IV had existed from his earliest years. In his horror of Victoria's 'wicked uncles' the Prince Consort determined that a central purpose of his eldest son's education should be to make him as unlike George IV as possible. Prince Albert's adviser, Baron Stockmar, pontificated at length on this topic and argued that the errors of the uncles had been of 'the most glaring kind, and we can find their explanation only in the supposition that their tutors were either incapable of engrafting on their minds during youth the principles of truth or morality, or that they most culpably neglected their duties…'[3] Many a busybody made free with similar advice, and the author of *Who Shall Educate the Prince of Wales?*, published in 1843, asked: 'Does not the conduct from boyhood to old age of George the Fourth point out the necessity for the most watchful attention to the education of him who is to reign over such a people?'[4]

Even without the George IV factor, considerable attention would undoubtedly have been given to the question of the education of Prince Albert Edward. Monarchs had for long enough agonized over how best to prepare their heirs for their weighty responsibilities, while high-minded Victorians were much preoccupied with the problems of education and the upbringing of children. Prince Albert was almost the archetype of such fathers and saw children as blank sheets on which could be imprinted the learning necessary to enable them to do their duty and pick their way through life's thorny path. Edward VII was only the most notable victim of a rigorous and unimaginative educational regime intended to produce a dutiful son in a father's idealized image.

Clearly, neither Prince Albert nor Baron Stockmar had bothered to look at the education George IV had received, for the irony is that the regime they devised for Prince

Throughout his life there were warnings and fears that Edward might follow in the footsteps of his 'wicked' great-uncle George IV, painted by Beechey while Prince of Wales in the uniform of the 10th Light Dragoons.

Albert Edward bore a close resemblance to it. George III had told the Prince of Wales's governor that he wished his sons to be brought up 'as examples to the rising generation' and the timetable laid down for the royal princes consisted of long hours of academic and moral instruction with intervals for exercise and dinner. The young George IV was strong-willed and, if his education did not make him a paragon of moral virtue, neither did it subdue his natural intelligence, and he grew up to be a well-read man with many intellectual interests and a love of art. Prince Albert Edward was less resilient than George, and if the Prince Consort and the tutors never succeeded in inculcating in him the character and virtues their system was intended to produce, they did nearly break his spirit, driving him from hysterical physical rebellion to a passive but sulky indifference. Neither as a youth nor as a man was Albert Edward ever openly to defy parental authority; he rather chose to circumvent and escape it. An enduring result of the Prince's education was that an intelligent and quick-witted man was rarely to pick up a serious book, and was to have time for only the lightest and most popular theatre. His restless search for pleasure and amusement can be accounted for as much by the boredom and depression of his childhood, as by Queen Victoria's refusal to give him any real responsibility.

Sovereigns, however much they may agonize over how best to prepare them for their future roles, are reluctant to give their heirs any real share of royal power or entrust them with actual responsibilities. Sir Francis Knollys, Edward VII's private secretary, considered the problem to be inherent in the nature of monarchy. 'It has been the same thing with Heirs Apparent from time immemorial, and I fear will continue to be so as long as there are monarchies'.[5] Albert Edward had to wait even longer than George IV until he succeeded to

Edward VII by Sir Luke Fildes. Certainly there were similarities between George and Edward, including their liking for display and costume.

the throne and the latter had at least been Regent in the decade before his accession. The greater part of the mature lives of both were spent as heirs apparent and neither was entrusted with serious duties. Like George, Albert Edward wished to follow a military career, but was not allowed to do so and had to be content with honorary colonelcies and the trappings of military life, although he was made a field marshal in 1895; in compensation he developed a rather absurd obsession with buttons and uniforms. Victoria resolutely turned down Gladstone's suggestion that the Prince should be made Viceroy of Ireland and refused him access to Cabinet papers and Foreign Office despatches for many years. He eventually received a key to the box containing Cabinet papers, owing to Disraeli's intercession, but had to wait until 1892 for a key to the Foreign Office despatch box.

What Knollys saw as the inherent reluctance of monarchs to share power with their heirs is unlikely to have fully accounted for Victoria's failure to give the Prince any real responsibility, although she was jealous enough of her position. There was, perhaps, a lingering fear that Albert Edward might, like the heirs to the first three Georges, associate with the political opposition, but to refuse him any share in constitutional duties was likely to have just that effect and, in any case, the declining political power of the monarchy took away much of the substance from such a fear. Victoria expressed the view that the Prince of Wales was indiscreet and was not to be trusted with secrets; indeed, he did like to gossip, but indiscretion comes easiest to those who have little to gain by discretion. It would seem that, in addition to the normal monarchical inclination to not yield an inch of authority while there was life in the body, the Queen had for much of her reign a pronounced distaste for her son. She was far from hating him, as, for instance, George II had hated Frederick, nor did she really dislike him. Indeed, in a rather distant way, she may have loved him, but he irritated her beyond endurance and offended her by being alive when the Prince Consort was not. Relations between Victoria and her eldest son did mellow as both grew older, and she gave him unstinting support when scandals threatened him, but she steadfastly refused to trust him with any share of her sovereign power.

The Prince of Wales was little suited to fulfil an Albertine role as patron of the arts and of progressive and worthy causes and institutions. He did, in fact, assume some of the posts filled formerly by his father and became President of the Society of Arts and Chairman of Wellington College. He was even appointed Chairman of the commission dealing with 'Albertopolis', Albert's own South Kensington development. He was also, in 1874, made a member of the Royal Commission on the Housing of the Working Classes, and later he became a member of the Royal Commission on the Aged Poor. But Albert Edward had little real interest in the arts and sciences, was easily bored by committee work and, although his quick sympathy was easily aroused by brief exposures to the poor and unfortunate, he lacked any reformist zeal. Fortunately Edward's wife, Alexandra, more than made up for these deficiencies. She actively involved herself in a wide range of charities; she was a regular visitor to the sick in hospitals and did much to advance the profession of nursing.

Victoria hoped that Edward's marriage in 1863 to the beautiful Princess Alexandra of Hesse-Cassel would have a steadying effect on him. Indeed, she 'looked to his wife as being HIS SALVATION'.[6] But it was not to be. Marlborough House, the home of Alexandra and Edward, immediately became the centre for fast and fashionable society, just as Carlton House had been in George IV's time. Certainly George and Albert Edward had much in common: both loved the company of women and had many mistresses; both were leaders of fashion and obsessed with clothes; if the one was the 'First Gentleman of Europe', the other became the 'Uncle of Europe' and a very convivial, roistering and jolly uncle he was; both liked cards and horse-racing; and both had gargantuan appetites for food and for life. They also had in common charm, kind-heartedness and loyalty to friends; on the other hand if George IV was the more cultured man, Edward had the common sense and restraint that George so conspicuously lacked. Edward had wit and, we are told, formidable powers of mimicry, although it is unlikely that in either he was in the same league as George.

If Marlborough House, like Carlton House in the late eighteenth and early nineteenth century, was the centre of society, there yet were important differences. George's delight in the arts, his original taste and quick mind, ensured that his circle included not only the well-born but writers, musicians, brilliant if dissolute politicians, and anyone who was amusing and original. Edward's world, too, was open to outsiders, those who had no automatic entrée to society, but these outsiders were men with money, often the *nouveau riche*: self-made men like Sir Thomas Lipton, the grocery magnate, and American and Jewish millionaires like W.W. Astor, Ernest Cassel and Baron Hirsch. If a symbiosis between wealth and birth, between plutocracy and aristocracy, was taking place in British society in the late nineteenth century, then the Prince of Wales hurried it along, and by the time he became King it had truly arrived. Philippe Julian described Edward as 'the incarnation not only of monarchy but also of capitalism'.[7]

As he became older, Albert Edward appeared to be happier in the company of these sorts of people than in that of the aristocracy. This was not an entirely new development. The

Princess Alexandra presents certificates to nurses at Marlborough House in 1899. It was Alexandra rather than Edward who gave practical encouragement to those who helped the sick and needy.

relationship between the Germanic royal family and the aristocracy had never been entirely comfortable. On the one hand, the fortunes of monarchy and aristocracy are intertwined as two hereditary entities, and the royal family are clearly at the head of society, in a position above the aristocracy – a position for long clearly underlined by royalty's policy of marrying royalty and educating royal children at home rather than allowing them to be educated alongside the indigenous upper crust. Yet there is also a sense in which the members of long-established and immensely wealthy aristocratic families have felt little awe for a German royal house which found its consorts in often rather shabby and impoverished foreign courts. Two of the scandals which dogged Edward's time as Prince of Wales were the result of aristocrats refusing to accept that his royal position was sacrosanct – Lord Randolph Churchill, when it appeared that Lord Aylesford was going to divorce his wife for her adultery with Churchill's elder brother, even challenged the Prince to a duel, and threatened to publish Albert Edward's indiscreet letters to Lady Aylesford if he did not intervene to prevent the divorce; and when Albert Edward took the side of Lady Brooke, Lord Beresford's ex-mistress, in her quarrel with Lady Beresford, Beresford is said to have actually hit the Prince of Wales. Of all Victoria's Prime Ministers, it was the most aristocratic, Lord Salisbury, who treated the wishes of both the Queen and her heir in the most cavalier fashion. Salisbury had little awe of majesty. When invited to Kaiser Wilhelm's yacht in 1895, he arrived one hour late and, when invited to return for a further visit the next day, he either misunderstood or forgot and did not arrive at all. In addition, he offended the Prince of Wales's punctiliousness in matters of dress by wearing the wrong trousers with a uniform jacket, excusing himself with the comment that 'It was a dark morning and I'm afraid that my mind must have been occupied by some subject of less importance'.[8]

If the Prince of Wales's character and personality grated upon the Queen, there is no doubt that it also upset an influential and voluble section of society – precisely that section that had come to approve of his father and which looked back with horrified fascination on what it saw as the self-indulgence and frivolity of the Regency. In addition, the constant attention of the press, free with criticism and advice, was becoming something that monarchy had to live with. Kilby Roby, in his *The King, The Press and The People*, has chronicled the constant carping and foreboding of many Victorian newspapers from the earliest stages of the Prince's life. Even his marriage was not sacrosanct. The *Evening Mail* argued in March 1863 that 'there had only been four marriages of the Prince of Wales in this country and that bad omens, vindicated by the results, surrounded them all'. The *Globe and Traveller* compared the Prince's marriage directly with that of George IV, 'not in the spirit of coarse censure of the past and still less in vain and overweening confidence in an unchequered future – never yet vouchsafed to man – but in the spirit of sober comparison of the two epochs'.[9] The succession of minor scandals which threw light upon the lifestyle and tone of the Prince's circle was pounced upon with delighted horror. The Tranby Croft affair, which concerned accusations of cheating against Lt-Col. Sir William Gordon-Cumming while playing baccarat with counters provided by the Prince at a house party in Yorkshire, gave press sanctimoniousness a field day, and the *New York Times* declared that 'The English people have no wish for a repetition of the court of George IV'.[10]

If the monarch's sole claim on society was as moral exemplar and a force for reform, progress and modernization, then, either as Prince of Wales or as King, Albert Edward doubtless did little to enhance it. Yet we must remember that Albert, the model for such a conception of the monarch's role, had not been popular outside the fairly narrow, though highly influential, section of society that was composed of the professions and the serious-minded and self-consciously respectable. Also, with all his worthy qualities and moral earnestness, he had never possessed those assets which were part and parcel of his eldest son's nature, namely charm and a combination of dignity and affability. Few crowds or individuals seem to have been impervious to these qualities. Albert Edward had the ability, since seen as an essential attribute of modern royalty, of at least appearing to enjoy the most boring or mundane of public occasions. Perhaps the secret is that he did enjoy them. He liked meeting citizens *en masse*, delighted in dressing up, and relished ceremony and parade. He was rarely at a loss for the apposite reaction or comment, whether opening a hospital in provincial Britain or sauntering in a foreign city. His charm was such that he was able to win over the erstwhile republicans, Sir Charles Dilke and Joseph Chamberlain, and the permanent republican Leon Gambetta.

Despite, or possibly because of, the condemnation by respectable members of society of his lifestyle, Albert Edward had a considerable popular following. Perhaps this was because the way he lived his life, the lavishness of which was admittedly a whole world away from that of ordinary working men and women, was one which was nevertheless comprehensible to them. He eagerly entered into the pleasures of horse-racing, gambling, drinking and the music hall, all of which were staple elements of late nineteenth century

King Edward with his horse Minoru, winner of the Derby in 1909. His love of the turf gave him at the same time a bond with the aristocracy and with the working classes.

popular culture. Against the background of this bawdy and hedonistic culture, though the periodic scandals that reverberated from the Prince's circle undoubtedly shocked many a respectable subject and activated wagging fingers in pulpits and the pens of leader writers, broad sections of the population remained unconcerned. Many of the working classes probably felt that there was little point in royal style and grandeur if some licence as to fleshly pleasures did not go with it, and echoed Bagehot's view that the role of the heir apparent was to taste 'all the world and the glory of it, whatever is most attractive, whatever is most seductive'.[11] Indeed, in one sense Edward's attraction was his capacity to err. As Lord Glanville said when he compared Edward with his father, 'Prince Albert was unloved because he possessed all the virtues which are sometimes lacking in the Englishman. The Prince of Wales is loved because he has all the faults of which the Englishman is accused'.[12]

After the death of his mother, and as her coffin was taken from the Isle of Wight to the mainland, the new king noticed that the royal standard on his ship was at half-mast and enquired the reason. On being told that it was because the Queen was dead, Edward replied: 'The King is alive'. At last, at the age of fifty-eight, Edward had come into his inheritance and he was determined to unshackle himself from the shadowy influence of his father and the very real dominance of his mother. The first evidence of this was when he quite deliberately chose to be called Edward, not Albert. He also made many changes at Windsor, ordering the removal of most of his mother's mementoes, especially those relating to John Brown. In most of the royal residences he embarked upon modernization schemes: new bathrooms and lavatories were built, the telephone systems were extended and some of the old coach-houses were converted into garages for motor cars.

King at last. Edward , chief mourner at Queen Victoria's funeral, walks alongside the Kaiser as the cortège passes through Windsor.

Above all, he was determined to be a magnificent and public king. Like George IV before him he had been a long time waiting in the wings, and now he was king he was determined to make the most of it. Time and self-indulgence had served him rather better than George and he was to enjoy nine very active years as king. He delighted in wearing splendid costumes, and loved public appearances – a satisfied enjoyment of his role is discernible in the paintings and photographs of Edward in his coronation robes. Edward was intent on showing other royal families what Britain and King Edward could do in the way of spectacle and ceremony. Nor was he content merely to be the central figure and allow the planning and organization of ceremony and display to be done by others. If the great impresario of royal ceremonies was Viscount Esher, Edward played a considerable part in devising them, and Esher himself admired Edward's 'curious powers of visualising a pageant'.[13]

This period has been interpreted as one in which the ritual of monarchy was, as part of a process of 'invented tradition',[14] made splendid, public and popular. But perhaps the notion of a 'renovation of tradition' is more apposite.[15] Large-scale royal ritual had ever been a necessary projection of monarchy: the novelty of the ceremonials at Victoria's Jubilees, in which Edward played a prominent part, and during his own reign, lay in the grand scale, the precision of the planning and the new context given by improved transportation, which allowed both a greater immediate audience and the attendance of foreign monarchs and imperial satraps. In addition, a mass circulation press and increasing numbers of illustrated and photographic magazines now allowed millions to attend these occasions vicariously.

Edward's first entry as sovereign into the City of London in October 1902. Edward delighted in public appearances, whether at the theatre or on more formal occasions.

Edward's public monarchy had been foreshadowed during the reigns of George III and George IV, and it differed from that of the Stuarts in offering not just monarchy itself, but monarchy as the focal point of national pride and loyalty. There was a general tendency during the nineteenth century, which has continued in the twentieth, for states to use ceremony and organized spectacle as a means of underlining and encouraging national cohesion and self-confidence. The German and Russian Empires also made a grand spectacle of monarchy, while republics like France and the United States staged ceremonies that glorified the state and its officials. It was perhaps the very fact that the British monarchy retained only residual political authority, and was increasingly seen as above politics, that made the exaltation of the institution synonymous with the exaltation of the nation in a way that most could accept. As its political power declined, so the British monarchy not only increased its social influence and popularity but acquired a quasi-sacerdotal status as the guardian and symbol of the national soul. It is tempting to see the refurbishment of the monarchy in the late nineteenth and early twentieth centuries as a self-conscious exercise born of the cynical insights of Bagehot and Disraeli; but the process may more realistically be viewed as a natural adaptation of a long-lived institution, one which always attempted to meet the psychological need of a populace to identify authority and legitimacy in a person and a family rather than in a mechanism. The rites of passage of monarchy were thus transformed into grand projections of those of ordinary subjects: the Jubilees, Victoria's funeral, the Coronation and funeral of Edward himself, the Coronation and Durbar of George V and the Investiture of the Prince of Wales, later

Edward VII and his first automobile. His love of tradition and uniformed splendour was complemented by his delight in new recreations.

Edward VIII. The pace of change also conferred certain attractions on an institution which was decreasingly part of the efficient side of the constitution: crowns, robes and gilded coaches stood out and gave a reassuring appearance of continuity in the age of motor cars and the telephone.

Edward's unique achievement was that while he so obviously loved dignified spectacle and ceremony, he also obviously delighted in more informal public occasions. Like so many of his subjects he enjoyed attending theatres and music halls, and nothing would prevent him missing the opening night of the new Gaiety theatre in October 1903.[16] Although he willingly participated in grand state visits abroad, it is unlikely that he got more pleasure from these than from his successes as a racehorse owner, especially his three wins in the Derby. Significantly, the last words that Edward is supposed to have uttered are 'I am very glad', a reply to his son who had just informed him that his horse, Witch of the Air, had won the 4.15 p.m. at Kempton Park.[17] It was this zest for the popular as well as the grand, and an enjoyment of the new while carefully maintaining traditions, which seemed to fit in exactly with the needs and desires of most of his subjects.

Lord Northcliffe's remark that Edward was 'the best king we ever had – on the racecourse', reflects the monarch's interest in the turf but it obscures an important aspect of his reign. In many respects Edward can be considered the first modern monarch, in that the limitations and possibilities of constitutional majesty, together with its expected functions, were either thrust upon him or developed by him. He was by no means acquiescent in the demise of royal political power but, save in foreign policy, was more concerned that the proprieties be observed than desirous of influencing political decisions.

More than any monarch since George II, Edward was at home in Europe and with European royalty.

He was supported by Knollys and Esher in his view that the King had the right to be formally consulted, and he wished to see Cabinet papers at the stage when policy was being formulated. This was a battle he would lose when the Conservative Prime Minister Balfour refused to agree. Edward grumbled but wisely gave in. In fact, the power of the royal prerogative diminished during his reign and it is noteworthy that it was at the hands of the Conservatives that it suffered most; relations between monarch and ministers were often indeed to be most strained, in the twentieth century, when the party of Church and King was in power.

There is considerable disagreement among historians, as there was amongst contemporaries, as to the influence Edward exerted upon foreign policy. Some have seen him as the architect of the *Entente Cordiale*, the 'uncle of Europe', maintaining a nepotistic control, while others have dismissed his influence as little more than useful public relations carried out under the strict supervision of ministers. Certainly he was seen by many European statesmen and commentators, particularly Germans, as exercising an enormous and Machiavellian influence. Edward knew Europe, where he spent several months every year, far better than most British politicians, and incomparably better than the insular Foreign Secretary, Sir Edward Grey. No other British monarch travelled so extensively on the continent or met foreign rulers so frequently, either on state or official visits or during his annual sojourns at Biarritz and Marienbad. The King was in a position to be influential and he definitely felt that he had a right to influence, but whether he exercised an independent sway is debatable. On the whole, his views on foreign affairs went with the grain of Foreign Office and Cabinet opinion, so that it is difficult to see whether he simply smoothed a path for government policy, or gave it a positive push. In any case, the fact that Edward's diplomatic efforts were exercised in harmony with government policy in no way belittles their importance.

Edward's last shooting party, during the visit of King Manuel of Portugal, November 1909.

Edward was a modern constitutional monarch, having at times to accept uncongenial ministers and policies of which he disapproved. Royal power and even prerogative were attenuated, and only in the circumstances of political crisis and impasse did residual power become significant. Such a crisis arose in the last year of the King's life. When it seemed likely that he would be called upon to create sufficient Liberal peers to allow the Parliament Bill introduced by the Liberal Government to pass the House of Lords, Edward considered inviting the Conservative leader, Arthur Balfour, to form an administration. Had he done so, this would have been the first time, since William IV called on Peel in 1834, that a sovereign had dismissed a government with a majority in the House of Commons. It was not to be, for Edward died before the decision had to be made.

Edward's greatest achievement, however, lay not in his incursions into political activity but rather in burnishing and repackaging the monarchy as a national symbol at once magnificent and popular. His good fortune here was that he had in general simply to be himself and to allow his natural inclinations a free run. Esher may have been the impresario and Elgar the musical director, but Edward was a natural star. He was dignified yet not pompous, plumed, uniformed and robed, yet modern and above all pleased with himself, his time and his people. He was a popular king: at his death a queue of 'six to eight abreast stretched seven miles to the entrance of Westminster, where his body was lying in State in William Rufus Hall' and at his funeral it was estimated that some two million people lined the streets of London.[18] Edward embodied a public monarchy as much at home in sacred national ceremonies as in more mundane visits to provincial towns, and he was perhaps lucky in that he ruled over a nation that was beginning to loosen its literal and metaphorical stays. He had been a Prince of Pleasure and the nation seemed to mind not at all when he became King of Pleasure. The shades of George IV and Lady Conyngham may well have looked with ghostly empathy, mingled with envy, at the cosy intimacy between Edward and Mrs George Keppel.

6 George V
Pomp and Respectability

> *He*:   Last evening
> I found him with a rural dean
> Talking of District Visiting…
> The King is duller than the Queen.
>
> *She*:   At any rate he doesn't sew;
> You don't see him embellishing
> Yard after yard of calico…
> The Queen is duller than the King.

(Max Beerbohm, *Ballade Tragique à Double Refrain*)

George V, both as a man and as a king, was dull. He was also rather decent in an irascible, fogeyish way. This combination of dullness and decency did much to gain him the affection of his people and to keep his throne when all about him were losing theirs.

His reign was a period in which the monarchy was, along with other institutions of British society, subjected to severe test. The British have tended to regard with some self-satisfaction the essential stability of their society and institutions during a period when other nations saw their kings depart, revolutions take place and radical and millenarian ideologies intrude. Some of this satisfaction may well be a complacency born of the facile hindsight of winners' history; if the crowds in front of Buckingham Palace on 11 November 1918 hailed the King who embodied the nation's perseverance, hardships and victory, things had looked very different a few months earlier when German armies were breaking through on the western front and the only monarchy to have tumbled was a British ally. There were troubles and problems enough for Britain and the monarchy throughout George's reign, from the constitutional crisis of 1910 to the slump of the 1930s. Yet there is considerable evidence that a deeply conservative social consensus enabled these problems to be surmounted.[1] That the King's character and personality mirrored that consensus was, at the least, apposite and may have done more to ensure its continuity than those historians who deny the importance of kings and queens care to admit.

Prince George was not expected to become king, and it was only on the death of his elder brother, Prince Albert Victor (Prince 'Eddy', later Duke of Clarence), in 1892 that he became second in line to the throne. In childhood and early youth, however, he and Prince Eddy enjoyed an identical upbringing and education. The Prince and Princess of Wales, unlike so many of their royal predecessors, loved all

'Three generations of naval men, the late King, the King and the Duke of Cornwall', is the caption of this Illustrated London News *photograph. Of the three, only King George was a professional naval officer.*

their children. The Princess probably lavished too much of her intense affection upon them and was reluctant to see them grow up and leave the hothouse of sentiment in which she brought them up. Harold Nicolson, George V's official biographer, wrote of her: 'Essentially she was a simple woman'.[2] She was beautiful, charming and kind but her main purpose in life appears to have been to recreate the innocent, domestic cosiness of her childhood in Denmark. As deafness made a wider social life more difficult, she withdrew into a closed world with her children and a few intimate friends. Prince George adored her in a style far removed from stiff understatement. At the age of twenty-three, the naval lieutenant wrote home, '… in about a month's time I shall see your beloved lovely face once more. Oh! Won't I give it a great big kiss and shan't we have lots to tell one another darling Mother dear after being separated for these long 7 months'.[3]

The Prince of Wales was the best of kingly fathers and was warm and indulgent towards his offspring. In later life, George V is supposed to have said, 'My father was frightened by his mother, I was frightened of my father, and I'm damn well going to see to it that my children are frightened of me', but we have Kenneth Rose's assurance that there is little reason to believe this anecdote[4] and it is controverted by almost everything we know about George's relations with his father. The Prince of Wales was a grand and imposing figure and, no doubt, a somewhat awesome one to a small boy, but he was relaxed and considerate with his son and treated him as a friend rather than a subordinate when he grew up. Edward would never have begun a letter to Prince

Albert as George did to his father, 'I cannot tell you how I miss you every minute of the day...'[5]

It is difficult to understand how George, whose relations with his parents were so warm and tender, became the stiff, gruff man who inspired fear and even dislike in his own children. A possible explanation is the sudden transformation in his life when in 1877 he and his brother moved from the arms of his adoring mother to the strictly disciplined and, at that time, harsh, uncomfortable world of the Royal Navy. Two years later George and Eddy set out on a three-year voyage around the world on the warship HMS *Bacchante*. They were accompanied by a tutor, the Reverend John Neale Dalton, a pretentious but kindly and conscientious man. While he secured the affections of both his charges, it cannot be said that his teaching met with much success, it had a negligible effect upon the backward Eddy and a very modest one upon George who remained deficient in the most elementary subjects. Thereafter the brothers parted. Eddy, being prepared for future kingship, went to Cambridge and then spent a period with the 10th Hussars, while George continued with his naval career.

To educate princes while they voyaged around the world was an imaginative enough project, but it casts some doubt upon travel's supposedly mind-broadening effects that George, the most widely travelled of British monarchs, was amongst the most insular in his attitudes. A naval career was not one which Queen Victoria favoured for an heir to the throne. She had opposed Prince Eddy joining:

> The very rough sort of life to which boys are exposed on board ship is the very thing not calculated to make a refined and amiable Prince... Will a nautical education not engender and encourage national prejudices and make them think their own country is superior to any other? With the greatest love for and pride of one's own country, a Prince and especially one who is some day to be its ruler, should not be imbued with the prejudices and peculiarities of his own Country, as George III and William IV were.[6]

There spoke the internationalism of an earlier generation, but the very prejudices Queen Victoria despised were to be useful to George in emphasizing the Britishness of the royal house in an increasingly nationalist world.

There can be little doubt that the death of the Duke of Clarence, whatever the personal loss to the royal family, was not an unmitigated tragedy for the British monarchy. Much is made of Eddy's dissipation, but his stupidity and listlessness were greater disqualifications for an heir to the throne. On his brother's death, George's life was completely reorientated. He gave up his career in the navy; he was created Duke of York; he was given his own household and two houses (part of St James's Palace and the Bachelor's Cottage at Sandringham which became, respectively, York House and York Cottage); and in July 1893 he married his dead brother's fiancée, Princess Mary of Teck. But, if the Duke of York was in almost every respect an improvement on the Duke of Clarence as a future king, he appeared to have considerable limitations of his own.

George had not been brought up as an heir to the throne and at the age of twenty-six his character, opinions, interests and abilities were firmly set. An attractive and affectionate boy had been transformed into a short, bearded and somewhat morose-looking man. He lacked the intellectual interests of his grandfather and the personal and social charm of his father. Life at sea within a narrow circle had given him set opinions, a mania for order and punctuality and a stiff social manner which hid an inner diffidence and narrowness. It had also developed a deep devotion to duty and the sturdy faith in British superiority that Queen Victoria so abhorred in a prince.

As Duke of York, George's timetable of public engagements was not onerous, and it allowed him to settle down to a pattern of life which the increase in commitments and pressure of work, as he succeeded to his father as Prince of Wales and then King, were to interrupt and inconvenience but not change. He is described by Nicolson as 'living the life of a country gentleman'[7] and according to Rose, 'He was essentially a countryman'.[8] If so, he was one of a new and growing breed of countrymen, quite unlike a great aristocratic landowner or even the 'Norfolk Squire' he has been likened to. He did not live in a great house or entertain in great style and he was not a leader of or even much of a participant in country society. His tastes inclined him to a house in the country rather than a country house. York Cottage was not large, so it excused him from having to entertain on any scale, there he could retire into a well-ordered and rigorously timetabled domesticity. The countryside was for pleasure, and at Sandringham, 'the place I love better than anywhere in the world',[9] George could refine his skill as one of the finest shots in the country, killing an enormous amount of game before spending an evening with his stamp albums and retiring to bed early.

With an unimaginative wish to spare his newly-wed wife the trouble, George had chosen the furnishings and decorations for York Cottage himself; the furniture came from Maple's and the popular pictures on the walls were reproductions. This unintentional slight is perhaps less surprising when set against the many invidious features of the Duchess of York's position. She had made a great match for a member of a somewhat indigent branch of the royal family, but she was not made welcome in the close circle of George's family. Princess Alexandra saw her daughter-in-law as a threat to her close relationship with her son and the Duchess had to bear many slights. George loved his wife but adored his mother and found it easier, at first, to express his feelings to her than his wife. The Duchess gained little comfort and support from her husband in her difficulties with his parents and sisters. But she did become a source of comfort to him and, in time, the marriage, which had taken place in contrived and inauspicious circumstances, was a success.

Recent writers, who have conceived of matriarchal heads guiding the destiny of the royal house,[10] have seen Queen Mary as a dominant figure, but this is too simplistic a view. She remained throughout her life in awe of her husband and his position. She zealously supported him, and subordinated herself, even in her dress, to his wishes. However, Queen Mary saw herself not just as the guardian of the King but of the institution of monarchy and, just as high priestesses can wield considerable power so, in a traditionally feminine way, did she.

A photograph of the Duke and Duchess of York at York House, St James's Palace. They preferred quiet evenings at home to society or lavish entertaining.

Mary was certainly a better wife than she was a mother. She exhibited little interest in her offspring when they were babies and although she became fonder of them as they grew older, she would rarely question the strict regime ordained by her husband, for he was king as well as father. Thus, at least between eldest son and father, the recurrent animosity that has distinguished that relationship in the royal house and which had disappeared for a generation was rekindled. Gaps between the generations have rarely been wider than in the 1920s, particularly between the 'old men' and younger men who had served in the War, while something of a cultural and moral war went on during the decade between the self-consciously modern who had to shock and the more sedate who were shocked. In this respect, the differences between the ultra-conservative King and that epitome of anti-stuffy modernity, the Prince of Wales, could stand for the conflict between thousands of fathers and sons throughout the land.

If George's relationship with his eldest son was strained, his relationship with his own father continued to be close throughout Edward VII's life. While his father was Prince of Wales, George received little induction into politics or affairs of state, but upon the death of Victoria this position changed. For the first time since the House of Hanover had acceded to the British throne, the heir was encouraged to prepare himself for the role that would one day be his. King Edward made sure, now that he at last was fully informed and consulted about political and diplomatic policy, that his son saw the most important Cabinet papers, and when George stayed at Windsor a writing table was provided for him next to the King's.

Yet when George succeeded his father in May 1910, contemporaries could have been forgiven for having doubts as to his fitness for the throne. It is true that he had comported himself with dignity in his public engagements and particularly during his visits to New Zealand, Australia, Canada and India. These imperial forays gave him an understanding and affection for the Empire that went beyond his father's, and his Guildhall speech, on returning from his 1901 tour, was a harbinger of what became a traditional role for princes as boosters of British trading interests while abroad and critics of industrialists and exporters at home. 'Wake up England' was to be translated into the less elegant 'Pull your finger out' of another sailor prince more than half a century later. But George lacked his father's presence and his intimate knowledge of European affairs. His political views also gave cause for concern, particularly as he could be voluble and indiscreet. He seemed very much a partisan Conservative and it had not been wise to tell the equally indiscreet Winston Churchill that Asquith was 'not quite a gentleman' or to refer to Lloyd George as 'that damn fellow', nor publicly to take the side of Lord Beresford in his dispute over naval strategy with Admiral Fisher. Once he was King, however, George did endeavour to keep his personal views to himself and he treated political adversaries with even-handedness.

George V's achievements were to go far beyond the modest expectations most contemporaries had of him. He accommodated the monarchy to the diminution of its control over political policy that had taken place over the previous reigns, without surrendering either its dignity or its position at the head of the state; he rescued it from the embarrassment of its continental connections and set a final stamp of

Englishness upon it; and he brought to his kingship an aura, at once domestic, imperial and majestic, that was in keeping with his time and which forged new links with every level of society. These were no mean achievements for a dull man.

He came to the throne without any great zest or appetite for kingship or any desire to play a dominant role in either domestic or European politics, and was thus inclined to a more muted and less assertive interpretation of the role of monarch than that aspired to by Edward VII. He also had a sturdy disregard for the type of public relations that later in the century would be considered essential for the monarchy. He had something close to contempt for the popular press and acceded only with great reluctance to the steady progress of the press barons up the ranks of the peerage. He read only *The Times*; the royal copy, like that produced for the copyright libraries, was still printed on linen paper. It was, perhaps, the inflamed chauvinism of the press during the First World War and the depths to which the 'anti-Hun' clamour descended that made George so contemptuous of the press. But earlier, to its credit, the British press had refused to allude to a recurrent but baseless rumour that George V was a drunk, or to repeat the assertions which appeared in the French newspaper *Liberator*, that George had been married, before his wedding to Princess Mary, to the daughter of a British admiral. The writer of this article, E.J. Mylius, was eventually prosecuted for criminal libel; during the trial, at the end of which Mylius was sentenced to a year's imprisonment, there was considerable public sympathy expressed for George, not only in Britain but worldwide. In view of the King's contempt for the manipulation involved in public relations, it is ironic to learn that his death was hastened by his doctor, influenced at least in part by pressure from the deadlines of the morning press.[11]

Paradoxically, it was with the newest of the mass media, the radio, that this conservative gentleman most easily came to terms. In the last years of his life he became a spectacularly successful radio broadcaster, with his Christmas day messages to the Empire. The first one in 1932, written for him by Rudyard Kipling, was an amazing success. It has been estimated that 20 million people listened to the broadcast and that something like 2,000 newspaper leading articles and 25,000 columns of newsprint were devoted to it throughout the world.[12] Thus was launched a national ritual which soon became a tradition. In 1934 the King's Christmas broadcast was described as 'the principal high-spot programme of the year'.[13] As Victoria and Albert had helped place the Christmas tree in the middle of the developing family-centred Christmas, so George ensured that Christmases after 1932 would be punctuated by a royal broadcast delivered not only to loyal families in Britain replete with turkey and good-will, but also to peoples throughout the Empire.

It is this growing emphasis on the Empire which most clearly distinguishes George's reign. As far as his ceremonial duties were concerned, George was content to follow doggedly in the footsteps of his father, who had done so much to create a new theatre of monarchy. In this respect, the Coronation and that new piece of pageantry, the Investiture of the Prince of Wales in 1911, should really be seen in the context of Edward's and Esher's innovations. George's kingship gained extra glitter, not in the further refurbishment of native tradition nor in the alien glamour of the royal association with European courts, but in concentrating on its imperial role. George's inclination had always been towards the Empire rather than Europe; his visits to the Dominions and the success of his Durbar in 1911-12 had encouraged this and it was in keeping with the post-war mood, as the Empire had stood so loyally by the mother country during the war. Of course, ever since the first day of 1877 when Queen Victoria proudly signed herself 'V.R. & I,' the monarch had been given an important imperial role. Indeed, it has been suggested that a major reason for the growing reverence for the monarchy during this period was its close identification as head of the Empire.[14] As the twentieth century developed, so too did the concentration on Empire. Although Empire Day had been celebrated before George came to the throne, it reached its peak of popularity during his reign. Robert Roberts recalled its centrality during his school days in Salford before the First World War.

> We drew union jacks, hung classrooms with flags of the dominions and gazed with pride as they pointed out those massed areas of red on the world map. 'This, and this, and this', they said, 'belong to us!' When next King George with his queen came on a state visit we were ready, together with 30,000 other children, to ask in song, and then... tell him precisely the 'Meaning of Empire Day'.[15]

In rural schools, the same sorts of activities were taking place. In Eynsham, Oxfordshire, Albert Ovenall remembered that Empire Day was always celebrated. 'Usually we were dressed to represent some part of the British Empire. We boys often dressed as sportsmen from those faraway places'.[16] The Empire Exhibition at Wembley in 1924 gave an even greater stimulus to imperial aspirations. The opening of the Exhibition by George V was the first important national event to be broadcast by the BBC, and the King's speech was transmitted 'all over the country'.[17] The connection between the monarchy and the Empire, especially at a time when the country was facing grave economic problems, not only added glamour to the monarchy but also, in Jeffrey Richards's words, gave the country an opportunity '... to rejoice in the essential soundness of Britain, her Empire and her institutions. The Empire thus moved with the monarchy above the narrow connotation of class and sectional interest to be seen as a symbol of the nation and thus an object of general patriotism'.[18]

It was understandable that after the ravages of the Great War Britain and its monarchy should look towards its Empire rather than towards a battered [6.3] Europe. The war had spotlighted grave social and economic weaknesses in the country, and for George V personally the war years, with their patriotic hysteria and Germanophobia, presented him with a number of embarrassing problems. One was the identification of the British Royal Family with their German ancestry, German relations and German names. George's naval upbringing had produced a very British king with no great enthusiasm for his European connections, but he did belong to the international caste of royalty. He was also a gentleman who believed in fair play. He was distressed by the hounding, by narrow-minded super-patriots, of such diverse individuals as Prince Louis of Battenberg, Lord Haldane and the members of Gottlieb's German Band, all of whom suffered in one way or another because of their German origins or connections. Less understandable and realistic was his dislike of the growing pressure for the enemy emperors, kings and princes to be deprived of their honorary commands of British regiments and their British orders of chivalry. He finally gave way, albeit reluctantly, to pressure from Asquith and Queen Alexandra to drop the names of royal foes from the Army list and from the roll of the Order of the Garter. But rumours and innuendoes concerning the royal connection with Germany continued. Lloyd George, who was never squeamish about hitting below the belt, remarked when summoned to the Palace in June 1915, 'I wonder what my little German friend has got to say'.[19]

In the spring of 1917 there was what appears to have been an orchestrated campaign against the King and the Royal Family, with a spate of letters arriving at 10 Downing Street asking how the Prime Minister could win the war when the King himself was a German. George V was at this time despondent and a little unnerved by the dethronement of his cousin, Tsar Nicholas, during the February Revolution in Russia. H.G. Wells's call for the abolition of 'an alien and uninspiring court' touched a raw nerve. 'I may be uninspiring but I'll be damned if I'm an alien' protested the King,[20] but he decided that a grand public gesture was required to impress upon the nation the British nature of the dynasty: the names of the Royal Family had to be anglicized. Lord Stamfordham came up with the inspired choice of Windsor as the new name for the royal house, although oddly enough nobody seemed quite sure what it was replacing: was the present family name Coburg, Guelph or Wettin? Windsor was, at any rate, redolent of English history and of a mighty castle. The junior members of the Royal Family also changed their names and dropped their foreign titles; thus Battenbergs became Mountbattens and Tecks, Cambridges. Also, the Titles Deprivation Act of 1917 relieved German princes such as the Dukes of Brunswick and Cumberland of their British titles.

Queen Victoria would undoubtedly have disapproved of this surrender to feverish war-time sentiment and would probably have sympathized with Kaiser Wilhelm's quip that he was going 'to the theatre to see the Merry Wives of Saxe-Coburg-Gotha'. The comment of Count Albrecht von Montgelas, that 'The true royal tradition died on that day in 1917 when, for a mere war, King George changed his name',[21] sums up the enormity of what had been done from the viewpoint of those who saw royalty as a caste who ruled over nations but were not part of such vulgar entities. Kenneth Rose has also suggested that the change of name occurred because of 'a momentary loss of nerve' by the King and that only a small minority of people within the country were really questioning the loyalty and patriotism of the Royal Family. Nevertheless, the changes were successful in underlining the British character of the dynasty. The episode was also an outstanding example of the invention of tradition: if one royal tradition had died, a new one had been born, and few of the subjects of George V's grand-daughter are aware that the House of Windsor has such a recent and undignified origin. That pressure on the throne of Britain had resulted in the anglicization of a family with scarcely a drop of British blood in it is demonstrated by

During the Great War, George V was constantly engaged in morale-boosting visits to army and naval bases and factories. Here, in the words of The Year 1918 Illustrated, *he ' acknowledges the gratitude of the Empire to some of those brave seamen'.*

a letter to George from his cousin Queen Marie of Romania, herself married into the Hohenzollern-Sigmaringen family: 'I can only tell you dear George that I held firm as only a born Englishwoman can'.[22]

George does seem to have felt insecure during the last years of the war. Nothing else can explain his rather heartless refusal to allow the Tsar of Russia and his family to take asylum in Britain. The British government was prepared to give refuge to the family but the King refused on the grounds that their residence in this country 'would be strongly resented by the public, and would undoubtedly compromise the position of the King and Queen'.[23] Of course, George could not foresee the fate that awaited the Russian Royal Family. Monarchs can display an ice-cold selfishness when they sense a danger to their throne and, in 1917, with the reverberations of the Russian Revolution having some impact on the British Left and a whiff of republicanism in the air, he felt that this was not the time to draw attention to his relationship with the Romanovs. That he felt guilty about his conduct later on is demonstrated by the uncharacteristic obstinacy with which he fought against having to receive a Soviet ambassador.

George V's role in the war was arduous but low key. He worked hard visiting army units and naval ports, hospitals and the manufacturing areas; he kept up with all the

A rare picture of George V smiling at the wedding of Princess Maud to Lord Carnegie in November 1923, one of three of his children to take British partners. He is chatting to his son the Duke of York, later George VI.

detailed information sent to him in his red boxes. He was not, however, a man to play the charismatic leader urging his people on to victory. He did his duty with a down to-earth common sense, and when someone remarked that a bombing raid on Buckingham Palace would have a stimulating effect on public opinion he, unlike his son and daughter-in-law twenty-five years later, answered 'Yes, but a depressing effect on me'.

One effect of the Great War was a savage diminution of the foreign dynasties it was politically tactful to marry into. The Royal Family now had to search elsewhere for marriage partners and the main source proved to be their own subjects. The marriage of Princess Louise to the Marquess of Lorne in 1871 had been the first marriage between the child of a sovereign and a subject to be given official sanction since the sixteenth century, but three of George V's children were to take British partners. These marriages strengthened the links between royalty and the aristocracy at a time when the economic, social and political position of the latter was undergoing a decline, but they built upon the change of dynastic name to Windsor and helped to make the Royal Family more British by blood as well as by adoption and more naturally in tune with the mores of the British upper classes.

George had himself reluctantly contributed to the decline in the political power of the aristocracy. Very soon after coming to the throne and during the constitutional crisis of 1910-11, he agreed, after receiving conflicting and inadequate advice from his two Private Secretaries, that if the Liberals won the next election he would create the necessary number of peers to secure the passing of a bill to curb the powers of the House of Lords. Just the threat of this (without the need to create peers) enabled a Parliament Act to be passed in 1911. The assurance respecting the creation of peers that George had given the Liberal leader Asquith was a momentous step, not only in the precedent it set for the use of the royal prerogative but also because, as an outcome, the powers of the Lords were permanently and severely restricted.

It appeared to many, in the circumstances of 1911, that a hereditary second chamber might not survive for long and would be replaced by either an elective substitute or a single chamber parliament. Yet although the membership of the House of Lords was later leavened by the life peerage system, hereditary peers continued to exercise their political rights until the end of the century. Some hereditary peers still sit in the Lords and the peerage in Britain continues to be a specific legal entity. That the British monarchy has not developed in the manner of its Scandinavian equivalents owes more than is commonly recognized to the continuation of the peerage and to the modernization of the honours system. That many, and some quite lowly, sections of society can hope that careers and public work may be rewarded with some place in a system of honours does much to bind society together, to focus attention on the monarchy as the official awarder of such distinctions and to lessen jealousy of the grandest titles and honours. The honours system was opened to wider sections of society in the later years of Victoria's reign (the Order of the Crown of India instituted in 1877 was, for instance, for ladies) and by Edward VII (Edward upgraded the Royal Victorian Order and in 1902 established the Order of Merit); but it was during George V's reign and during the Great War that the most democratic order, that of the British Empire, was founded and businessmen, social and charitable workers and even trade unionists admitted to its ranks. Lloyd George's manipulations may have abused the honours system and some of his 'dreadful knights' may not have been conspicuously worthy, but a widened honours system strengthened aristocracy and monarchy and was a factor for social stability.

The King tried hard to be cautious and a conciliator when it came to politics. Nicolson has commented on George's conception of his role:

> His faith in the principle of Monarchy was simple, direct even; but selfless. All that he aspired to do was to serve that principle with rectitude; to represent all that was most straightforward in the national character; to give the world an example of personal probity; to advise, to encourage and to warn.[24]

Elizabeth Longford has referred to George as 'The first great constitutional monarch'[25] but he was not that; rather, his reign marked a new stage in the evolution

A photograph of George V at the time of his Jubilee.

of constitutional monarchy. The prerogatives were retained and the monarch continued to be informed by his governments, but personal influence upon government policies was much diminished. The political responsibilities which remained were largely those to be exercised at times of political impasse – granting or withholding requests for the dissolution of Parliament, and calling upon political leaders to form governments. That George V did play an important political role was due to the fact that such times were frequent during his reign. The norm of British political life is supposed to be government by a single party with an overall majority, but the 'norm' only prevailed for six years of the reign. A more assertive and more ambitious, perhaps even a more confident, monarch could have used recurrent political crises to have maintained great personal political influence, but it would have been a dangerous game. As it was, a warm human sympathy and a practical concern for his throne and the stability of his kingdom informed his attitudes. He had always had a good naval officer's concern for the men under his command; troubled acutely by the ordeal servicemen had gone through during the Great War, he came also to realize how badly many of them were rewarded in a post-war world characterized by national economic decline, unemployment and industrial unrest. His approach to

King George and Queen Mary leave Crathie church after attending a service during the King's last holiday at Balmoral in 1935.

such major post-war problems as Ireland and the General Strike was to urge reconciliation and restraint. Independence for the South of Ireland was a blow, because he had always believed that the Crown had a special relationship with the people of the South as well as of Northern Ireland, but he could find some comfort in the fact that the Free State remained within the Empire. Like the majority of the nation, George condemned the General Strike, but he had sympathy for the rank-and-file of the strikers, and perhaps his most constructive action was the lead he gave in accepting the Labour Party and Labour governments as a normal feature of the body politic.

The most conservative of British monarchs, George never had any time for the ideological aspirations of the Labour Party, but he had some sympathy for the circumstances and conditions of labour and got on well with many members of Labour cabinets, particularly those who had risen from humble backgrounds. Clement Attlee said of him, 'He knew and understood his people and the age in which they lived, and progressed with them'.[26] Although the King was reluctant to accept change, so also was much of the nation, and there was much that was conservative about the working-class leaders of the Labour Party. It was his determination to be even-handed between political parties that led George to favour inviting Ramsay Macdonald to form a government in 1924. After swearing in Macdonald, George wrote in his diary, 'I had an hour's talk with him, he impressed me very much; he wishes to do the right thing. Today 23 years ago dear Grandmama died. I wonder what she would have thought of a Labour government'.[27] Eleven years and several ministries later, George wrote to Macdonald after receiving his resignation as Prime Minister: 'You have been the Prime Minister I have liked best; you have so many qualities, you have kept up the dignity of the office without using it to give you dignity'.[28]

George's sympathy for working people was reciprocated. Malcolm Muggeridge contended that George V was more popular with the lower classes than he was with the upper,[29] and George Orwell was forced to admit that the affection shown for the King at the Jubilee was:

> …obviously genuine, and it was even possible to see in it the survival or recrudescence of an idea about as old as history, the idea of the King and the common people being in a sort of alliance against the upper classes, for example, some of the London slum streets bore during the Jubilee the rather servile slogan 'Poor but Loyal'. Other slogans, however, coupled loyalty to the King with hostility to the landlord, such as 'Long live the King. Down with the landlord'.[30]

Other commentators have asserted that George V made a special appeal to the middle classes but it would be truer to conclude that he appealed to middle Britain, to the great majority of the population who, whether country gentry, suburban middle class or working class, valued conservatism, respectability and stability. As James Pope Hennessy has written,

> The reign of King George V witnessed violent social and other upheavals. Throughout all these, the Monarchy remained stable, safe and an example of old-fashioned rectitude and simplicity. King George subconsciously realised that to be stable in so public a position is not enough, one must look stable as well.[31]

George had little time for highbrows although, as he always thought the word was 'eyebrows', he was probably a little puzzled as to what they were. In Rose's brilliant sentence, he '…liked a book with a plot, a tune he could hum and a picture that told a story'.[32] In this he was like ninety-nine per cent of his subjects – indeed, the monarchy will probably be at its most vulnerable if a monarch should ever appear who reads the contemporary equivalent of *Finnegan's Wake*, listens to atonal music and likes abstract art.

There is no doubt that by the end of his reign both George and the institution of monarchy were popular. A survey of newsreels, taken in 1936, showed that items featuring royal events were the most popular after sport: 'Queues formed outside cinemas everywhere' to see the newsreels of the Jubilee celebrations.[33] A mere Silver Jubilee had never been celebrated before, and although it was probably partly true, as some critics observed, that these celebrations were encouraged by the National government to enhance its own popularity, the fact was that the countrywide rejoicings exceeded all expectations.

A king who had never courted popularity, rarely smiled on public occasions, and had simply been content to do his duty and serve the institution of monarchy, found to his own considerable surprise that he was enormously popular with all classes. The tremendous display of affection, at the time of the Jubilee, for this conventional old man who accepted the modern world with reluctance and some distaste, who had his domestic difficulties like everybody else and who had spent much of his life-time dealing with 'those damned politicians' amazed him. 'I'd no idea they felt like that about me', he said.[34]

7 The Sons of George
A Question of Duty

The image and style of the monarchy seemed certain to change with the accession of Edward VIII to the throne. As Prince of Wales, Edward had proved a popular and glamorous figure, not only in Britain but throughout the Empire and the many countries he had visited, on the frequent royal tours he had made since the ending of the First World War. He was not only the first royal 'superstar' but one of the great superstars of the twentieth century. He photographed well and his image seemed to contemporaries to represent the modern spirit of the age. His handsome, well-tailored appearance, together with his obvious personal charm and his liking for parties and a smart circle of friends, made a stark contrast to the stuffy, old-fashioned country gentleman image presented by his father George V. In addition, his seeming concern for the underprivileged and his impatience with many of the traditions associated with the monarchy and Court circles, suggested that the new king intended to be not only popular but innovative.

Right from the start, in fact the day after his father's death on 20 January 1936, Edward signalled that the monarchy was being hurried into the modern age. He eschewed more traditional forms of transport and flew from an airfield near to Sandringham to Hendon, in order to attend his Accession Council at St James's Palace. There is no doubt that Edward wanted to appear as 'the people's King' and that he wished to do away with much of the protocol and what he believed to be the outdated duties which he was asked to perform. It was over issues such as these that he had disagreed frequently with his father. During the War Edward had protested to his father, but without success about being forced to wear military medals which he felt he did not deserve. But while this sort of attitude angered George V, Edward's egalitarianism and his desire to share the conditions experienced by the troops made him a very popular figure. A private who had fought through the Battle of the Somme recalled the time towards the end of the war, when 'we were so fed up we couldn't even sing 'God Save the King' on Church Parade. Never mind the bloody King, we used to say, he was safe enough, it should have been God save us. But we worshipped the Prince of Wales'.[1] Edward's popularity with servicemen was highlighted again in 1919 while on his visit to Canada, when thousands of ex-servicemen broke ranks at a parade in order to cheer and congratulate him.

The relationship of George V to his eldest son resembled that of most Hanoverian fathers and sons. Time and again they clashed. George complained about Edward's often flippant attitude towards ceremonies and Court procedures, he despised his dress-sense, detested his friends and thoroughly disapproved of Edward's penchant for married women. Later, in his autobiography, Edward was to write that his father 'disapproved of Soviet Russia, painted fingernails, women who smoked in public, cocktails, frivolous hats, American jazz, and the growing habit of going away for weekends'. Edward added that 'While I shared in my father's distrust of communism, I couldn't see anything glaringly

The Prince of Wales was popular wherever he went on the Western Front. Here he is with Field Marshal Haig on Armistice Day.

reprehensible about the others'. Above all, however, what irritated Edward about his family was 'the relentless formality of their lives'.[2]

Despite these conflicts at home, Edward remained an immensely popular public figure. His tours to the Dominions and his visits to the poorer parts of Britain, where he so often showed concern and interest, established him as the royal favourite of both the population and the press.

Popularity alone could not ensure that the nature of the monarchy would change overnight. At a time when Britain's position as a world power, both in the economic and political sense, was declining, many politicians believed that the monarchy had an essential role to play in keeping the Empire together. This role necessitated a monarch who was prepared to fulfil all its functions and who would not challenge procedures and policies. Coupled with this opinion were the views of an influential old guard, which had included George V himself, who continually reminded Edward that he must remember his position and maintain the dignity of the monarchy. Their adherence to the nineteenth-century view of monarchy as interpreted by Bagehot was complete. As Sir Frederick Ponsonby, who had served under the three previous monarchs, pointed out to Edward, 'there is risk in your making yourself too accessible… The monarchy must always retain an element of mystery… The monarchy must remain on a pedestal'.[3] Another pillar of the Establishment, J.C.C. Davidson, also recorded that he was doubtful whether Edward would 'make a King in the same class as King George V, who was a man of the highest character and sobriety and a devoted husband'. Davidson claimed he reached this conclusion in 1912 when the two men first met. Even then he 'did not quite like the personality of the Prince of Wales, charming in some ways as he was… From then onwards, studying the Prince of Wales and meeting him from time to time, I formed the conclusion that he was an obstinate, but really a weak man, in whose pastimes I could have taken no share, and whose friends, male and female, I would not wish to have known intimately…'[4]

It is difficult to estimate to what extent Davidson's views were built on hindsight, and to know exactly what he meant when he concluded that Edward was essentially a weak man. It is true that, although throughout his life Edward was well-liked by many of his colleagues, he was not always able to compete with them intellectually. As a boy cadet, Edward, like his younger brother Bertie, never came far from the bottom of the class during his stay at the Royal Naval College. Later, when he was a student at Magdalen College, Oxford, the Master of that College diplomatically and with total understatement said of the Prince that 'bookish he will never be'. Despite all his charm, Edward was a lonely and moody man. He would often and suddenly suffer fits of depression and, despite his views on the role and image of the monarchy, it is arguable whether he had the intellectual stamina and commitment to pursue his ideas to the very end. It became clear, soon after he became King, that Edward was skimping on a number of specific royal duties. State papers which were delivered to him were returned sometimes weeks late, and often there was no evidence to show that he had even glanced at them. As Edward later admitted, 'This interminable amount of desk work was all the more taxing for me because, if the truth must be known, I have never had much zeal for paper work'.[5] One other important factor which distracted him from these sorts of duties, and of which the British public was unaware at this time, was that Edward was desperately in love with the twice-married Mrs Wallis Simpson. In the words of his Assistant Private Secretary, 'It was she who filled his thoughts at all times, she alone who mattered, before her the affairs of state shrank into insignificance'.[6]

Although not beautiful, the witty and elegant Bessie Wallis, the American wife of Ernest Simpson, a shipping broker, was by 1934 Edward's closest companion. Edward, in his autobiography, stated that he admired Wallis for 'her forthrightness' and 'from the first I looked upon her as the most independent woman I ever met'.[7] Two years younger than Edward, Wallis nevertheless was much more mature and was the dominant partner. This is reflected in their correspondence, which resembles 'letters exchanged between a fond but wise parent and a lonely, hypersensitive child at boarding- school'.[8] Edward, in his relationships with women, appeared to prefer sometimes older and often married women. Viscountess Coke was twelve years older than he, Mrs Dudley Ward, although a year younger, was married, as was Thelma Viscountess Furness. But by 1934 both Mrs Dudley Ward and Lady Furness had been firmly replaced by Mrs Simpson as Edward's favourite.

The fact that this most eligible of bachelors was enamoured of a twice-married, American, commoner, horrified leading members of the Church, many politicians and, of course, George V and the rest of the Royal Family. His mother's attitude towards divorce

Mrs Wallis Simpson. 'Before her the affairs of state shrank into insignificance.'

was starkly simple. 'One divorce could seldom or never be justified, and to divorce twice, on any grounds whatsoever was to her unthinkable'.[9] But Edward was determined to continue with the relationship, and while it was something which perhaps could be tolerated while he was Prince of Wales, matters were bound at some point to come to a head once he became King.

Meanwhile, the British public remained in ignorance of Edward's romance and the trouble that loomed ahead. He was depicted in both the press and the newsreels as a hardworking King whose visits to Clydeside and the Rhondda valley were illustrative of his concern for the unemployed living in depressed areas. Even when, during the summer of 1936, Edward went for a cruise with Mrs Simpson on board the yacht *Nahlin*, the British media made no mention of her, and the King was portrayed as a man who was taking a 'well deserved rest from the cares of state'.[10] Geoffrey Dawson, the editor of the *Times*, writing later about the role of the press during this period, declared that it was not subjected to 'censorship nor collusion... The nearest approach to interference from high quarters was probably the customary request from Buckingham Palace (as old as Queen

Victoria) that the Sovereign's privacy should be respected by the Press during the annual holiday abroad'.[11] But while the British media remained silent on the subject, American and European newspapers were full of the romantic affair and the progress of the two lovers on holiday along the Dalmatian coast.

Despite the news blackout it was impossible to prevent rumours spreading, and on returning to his office in early October 1936, after a two months absence owing to ill-health, the Prime Minister, Stanley Baldwin, was alarmed at the amount of the correspondence on this subject that awaited him. Up until this point Baldwin had not approached the King to discuss Mrs Simpson, despite the many urgings from some of his Cabinet colleagues. Now he was forced to take some action, especially as he was also informed that Mrs Simpson was suing for divorce and that her petition was to be heard at Ipswich Assizes on 27 October. The consequences of a successful suit would mean that after six months, when the decree nisi became absolute, this American with two divorced husbands still living would be in a position to marry the King of England.

Edward, along with his close friend Walter Monckton, approached the newspaper magnates Lord Beaverbrook and Esmond Harmsworth, who agreed that while they would report on the divorce suit, they would not comment on it or link Edward's name with Mrs Simpson. To this end, they also met and secured the consent of the other newspaper proprietors.[12] But Edward was not so successful in persuading his Ministers to accept Mrs Simpson and although the press in a most gentlemanly fashion agreed to remain silent, from October to early December, the future of the King was debated behind closed doors. Meanwhile, in public, it was business as usual with the King performing his state duties of opening Parliament, taking part in the Remembrance Day service at the Cenotaph, visiting the Home Fleet and making a tour of South Wales.

As the public was unaware of Edward's desire to marry Wallis Simpson, it is impossible to assess just how much popular support Edward would have received for such an action, but the Government, most of the Labour opposition and, of course, the Church of England led by Archbishop Lang, were determinedly against it. Even when a morganatic marriage was proposed, the idea was vetoed by the Cabinet and the response which came from the Prime Ministers of the Dominions was equally unfavourable. Edward was eventually presented with three alternative lines of action. Either he renounce Mrs Simpson, or he marry her contrary to the advice of his Ministers who would then resign. This latter course would cause a serious and unprecedented constitutional crisis, as the leaders of both the Liberal and Labour parties had pledged to Stanley Baldwin that they would not form an alternative government in such an event. The third alternative remaining to Edward was abdication.

Towards the end of November it became clear that press silence could not be maintained for much longer, and on 3 December the story of Edward and Wallis Simpson was broken to the country at large. In his diary for that day 'Chips' Channon recorded: 'The Country and the Empire now know that their Monarch, their young King-Emperor, their adored Apollo, is in love with an American twice divorced, whom they believe to be an adventuress'.[13] While the press speculated about the future of the King, Edward remained determined to marry Wallis Simpson and to this end was prepared to give up the throne. Finally, on 10 December, Edward signed the Instrument of Abdication. The following day

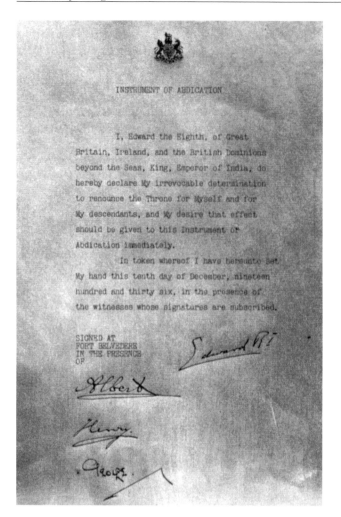

The Instrument of Abdication, signed by Edward VIII and witnessed by his brothers.

he broadcast to the nation stating that he could not carry out his duties as King without the support of the woman he loved. That same night Edward, now Duke of Windsor, was driven to Portsmouth where he crossed to Europe on the destroyer HMS *Fury*.

Throughout the crisis Stanley Baldwin had feared that the criticisms to which the monarchy was exposing itself might result in irreparable damage to the institution. He was also concerned that a 'King's Party' might spring up in Edward's defence. For a few days in December small crowds, especially in London and outside Buckingham Palace, did make themselves heard in proclaiming their loyalty to Edward. Both Fascists and Communists attacked the government for its attitude towards Edward and in addition, for a short time, it seemed possible that a section of the press and a number of MPs led by Winston Churchill might pursue Edward's cause. Edward, in his autobiography, argued that there was strong support within the country for him at the time of the Abdication, but it remained quiescent because he himself made no move to encourage either the press or the public to protest. 'If I had made an appeal to the public I might have persuaded a majority and a large majority at that… there is no want of evidence that a multitude of the

The King who was never crowned. A commemoration flag for the coronation that never was.

plain people stood waiting to be rallied to my side'.[14] Nevertheless, there were many who believed that Edward should forget Mrs Simpson and do his duty as a monarch. 'The Nonconformist Conscience in England was not dead'.[15] For others the episode was of little importance, merely one of interest and amusement. Evelyn Waugh recorded in his diary that 'The Simpson crisis has been a great delight to everyone. At Maidie's nursing home they report a pronounced turn for the better in all adult patients. There can seldom have been an event that has caused so much general delight and so little pain'.[16]

It is difficult to agree with Lord Beaverbrook's statement that as a result of the Abdication, 'Without doubt, the throne trembled'.[17] If anything, the episode reflected the resilience of the institution and it emerged virtually unscathed. Parliament remained loyally in favour of the monarchy and when the leader of the Independent Labour Party, James Maxton, moved an amendment to the Abdication Bill proposing that the monarchy and the hereditary principle should be abolished, it was defeated by 403 votes to 5. What the Abdication crisis did expose was the essential vulnerability and weakness of the monarchy when once it was confronted by both the Establishment and the politicians. Edward's predecessors had had the good sense never to manoeuvre themselves into the position he found himself in, but although he was no Machiavelli, the ease with which he was defeated came as a shock, if not to him, certainly to his more able but bewildered future wife. 'Nothing that I had seen had made me appreciate how vulnerable the King really was, how little power he could actually command, how little his wishes really counted for against those of his Ministers and Parliament. David did nothing to disabuse me of these misconceptions. And, too, right to the end it seemed utterly inconceivable to me that the British people and the Dominions would ever allow anybody who had served and loved them so well to leave them'. [18]

From 1937 onwards Edward was an acute embarrassment to successive governments and to the new King, although he retained the affection of many people. To the unemployed miners of Brynmawr whom he insisted on meeting in 1936, he remained a folk hero, and on the few occasions when he returned to Britain inevitably a crowd gathered to cheer him. After his death in 1972, when his body was brought back to Windsor to lie in state, 57,000 people filed past his coffin in order to pay their respects. [19]

The behaviour of the media over the Abdication and the accession of George VI was remarkably restrained and courteous. One hundred years before, in similar circumstances, the monarchy would have been attacked mercilessly. But then the monarchy had been seen as possessing considerable political power, while by the 1930s it was considered to be above the fray of party politics. It was as important an institution as ever but was essentially perceived as the symbol and focus of national unity, not an attractive target for caricature.

The main task in 1937 was to present Edward's successor, his younger brother Bertie, to the public and to remould the image of the monarchy. In order to achieve this the British media deliberately chose to ignore the Duke of Windsor, who was now living on the Continent. Indeed, the chiefs of the five largest newsreel companies mutually agreed that the wedding of the Duke to Mrs Simpson, which took place on 3 June 1937, should be 'barred from every screen in Britain'. [20] It was Bertie and his family who were now pushed into the limelight. Baldwin, who had been contemplating retirement, decided to stay until after the Coronation in May 1937 in order 'to see the new King into the saddle'. [21] But even before Edward actually abdicated, the editor of *The Times* told one of his staff to write a piece on the Duke and Duchess of York who were returning to London from Scotland. This was 'the opportunity you've been waiting for to try and spread the loyalty of our readers a little more widely over the Royal Family'. [22] Newsreel companies too hastened to prepare the public for a new monarch. In the case of Gaumont British one newsreel item and script entitled 'Our New King and Queen' was prepared before it was known by what name the new king would be called. After remarking on the popularity of the Duke and Duchess and the two princesses, Elizabeth and Margaret Rose, the script of the news item concluded, 'In the hands of King Albert we may rest assured that the dignity of the Crown, so well established by his beloved father King George V, is in safe keeping- and to King Albert and Queen Elizabeth we wish long life, happiness and courage in the years to come. God Bless Them'. [23]

The media now focused its attention on the new king and his family and relations to an unprecedented extent. Of the 101 newsreels made by Movietone News in the year following the Abdication, there were eighty-nine items concerning members of the Royal Family. (Only two of these items involved the Duke and Duchess of Windsor). In the previous year, despite newsworthy events such as the death of George V and the accession of Edward, there were only forty-three items connected with royalty screened in a similar number of newsreels. [24] The Royal Family were regularly depicted as a united family going about their duties happily and honourably. After the saga involving a king's liaison with a married woman and a divorce suit, it was felt necessary now to play the game of happy families. Another reason why the emphasis was put on the family as a whole was that there were some doubts about George's ability. He was a quiet, nervous man, with a noticeable speech impediment and a history of poor health. Also, unlike any other previous British monarch, he was given at the very most three weeks' notice that he might have to be King. Understandably in these circumstances he had his own doubts about his ability to fulfil the role which he found thrust upon him. He told Lord Louis Mountbatten, 'I'm quite unprepared for it. David has been trained for this all his life. I've never even seen a state paper; I'm only a naval officer, it's the only thing I know about'.[25]

Even as a naval officer Bertie, as he was known, had not met with much success. In his first year at naval college he came sixty-eighth in a class of sixty-eight, and when he left Dartmouth at the age of seventeen had only risen to sixty-first out of a class of sixty-seven.[26] To cap it all, when he undertook his first tour of duty in 1913 he was desperately seasick. During the War he was stationed at Scapa Flow and he did see some action at the Battle of Jutland; but he suffered from gastric troubles and in 1917 a duodenal ulcer, for which he underwent an operation, forced him to leave the Navy. So, while his elder brother was being praised by the British troops for his work on the Western front, Bertie's wartime experiences were less publicized. This conformed to an established pattern: invariably it was David who received the headlines while Bertie spent most of his early life in David's shadow. As one of his tutors once remarked, comparing Bertie with David 'was rather like comparing an ugly duckling with a cock pheasant'. But although this ugly duckling may not have been transformed into a swan, he did develop into a hardworking, earnest and useful member of the Royal Family. Much of the credit for this must go to Elizabeth Bowes-Lyon, who was finally persuaded to marry Bertie in 1923. In many ways, the relationships between Bertie and Elizabeth, and Edward and Wallis Simpson, were similar. Elizabeth was much more mature than Bertie and he 'was almost entirely dependent on the Queen whom he worshipped: she was his will power, his all'.[27] Both Elizabeth and Wallis Simpson were strong-minded, determined women, and perhaps it was because they were so similar in character that they detested each other so heartily. However, there was one extremely important difference in the two marriages. Unlike that of Edward and Wallis, the marriage of Bertie and Elizabeth received total approval from George V and Queen Mary.

Three years before his marriage Bertie was created Duke of York. With that honour came duties, but whereas Edward's role was the glamorous one of unofficial royal ambassador to the Dominions, Bertie had the task, albeit an important one, of meeting the industrial workers of Britain. Between 1920 and 1935, a period marked by industrial tension and depression, he visited some 120 to 150 factories around the country, earning himself the nickname of 'the foreman' within his family. It was a duty which he took very seriously and although he was powerless to effect many changes, he did, in his own way, try to break down some class barriers. Working with the Industrial Welfare Society, he was largely responsible for the setting up of annual boys' camps in which public schoolboys could mix with boys from working-class homes. These 'Duke of York's camps', as they came to be known, were held from 1921 to 1939; as well as helping to organize the camps, Bertie invariably spent (apart from 1934 when he was ill) at least one day at each camp taking part in the day's activities.

What endeared him most to the British public was his image as a family man, the father of two pretty young daughters and the husband of an attractive and charming wife. It was

The attractive and ever popular Elizabeth Bowes-Lyon, the new Queen.

this asset, more than any other, which made Baldwin and others believe that despite the upheavals of Edward's brief reign, the continuity of the monarchy would be assured. After the glitter and superficial sophistication of Edward and his circle, there was need to return to the solidarity and stability exemplified by the reign of George V. So it was no accident that the new king was also named George, a final blow to Queen Victoria's hope that the name Albert would become intimately associated with the monarchy. It was a role the Duke of York could perform. For although, as with his brothers, his relationship with his father had at times been a very uneasy one, in some ways he was similar in character to George V. As the Duke of Windsor wryly pointed out, 'The patterns of their lives were much the same, with the steady swing of habit taking them both year after year to the same places at the same time and with the same associates… Both were devoted family men, a quality that goes a long way for a King in a constitutional monarchy'.[28]

Again, after the fiasco of Edward's reign, it was agreed that much should be made of the Coronation of the new king. Some £454,000 was expended on it, about two and a half times as much as that spent on George V's. Not only money but much care was taken to ensure that the occasion was a great and well-organized spectacle. The Earl Marshal, the Duke of Norfolk, insisted on eight rehearsals before the actual ceremony took place, and perhaps even more important, he and the Archbishop of Canterbury were given the power to edit all photographs and newsreel films of the event. In addition to full newspaper and newsreel coverage there was, for the first time, radio presentation of a coronation. Microphones were taken into Westminster Abbey and the ceremony was heard throughout the country.[29]

The Coronation, attended by representatives from all the Dominions, was a splendid and sumptuous affair. It was an unashamed attempt to depict the unity of the Empire and the strength and stability of the titular head of that Empire, at a time of increasing international unrest. In this sense, it was not markedly different in conception from that of the Coronation of George V. What was new was the time and space spent by the media, not on the monarch, but on the Royal Family in general and the two young princesses in particular. If the reign of George VI contributed anything to the development of the social influence of the monarchy in this country, it was in its depiction of the monarch as father as well as King – as the head of a family which, although royal, shared the typical hopes, joys and concerns of respectable families throughout the nation.

The Times commented at the time of the Coronation that the ceremony marked 'the dedication once more of the Sovereign and the whole Royal Family to the nation's well-being'.[30] Duty was the key issue confronting the Royal Family. It was an issue easily understood. Queen Mary had never comprehended how her eldest son could ignore his duty. As she wrote to him in 1938, 'All my life I have put my Country before everything else, and I simply cannot change now'.[31] George was cast in his mother's mould and his dedication to duty was best manifested during the years of the Second World War. Conscientiously, the Royal Family remained in London during much of the blitz and they were invariably depicted in the media as just another family bravely facing war on the Home Front. When on 13 September 1940 Buckingham Palace itself was hit, the News Division of the Ministry of Information immediately went into action. 'Arrangements were made for more than 40 journalists… to visit the Palace to see the damage. The theme 'King with His People in the front line' was stressed… The story was front page news throughout countries outside the Axis orbit'. The head of the News Division claimed that this event, 'immediately dissipated bad feeling in the East End, led to remarkable expressions of affection for the Royal Family and aroused intense indignation throughout America'.[32] Queen Elizabeth may well have shared this feeling, for she was reported to have said, 'I'm glad we've been bombed: it makes me feel I can look the East End in the face'. In fact, it was the example set by Queen Elizabeth which most often caught the public eye and impressed those who met her. Her reply, when asked whether the Royal Family would seek safety abroad, is well known: 'The children can't go without me. I can't leave the King, and of course the King won't go'.[33] Again, in a letter dated 10 July 1940, Harold Nicolson reported on a conversation he had with the Queen in which she informed him that she was undergoing instruction in revolver shooting each morning, for

'The King with his people in the front line'. King George and the Queen inspect the damage at Buckingham Palace after a bombing raid in September 1940.

she was determined not to 'go down like the others'. Nicolson was moved to add, 'I cannot tell you how superb she was'.[34]

All the members of the Royal Family made their contribution to the war effort. The King himself was urged, and reluctantly agreed, to help cement unity in the country and the Empire by reinstituting the Christmas Day broadcasts made so popular by his father. Fully aware of his speech defect, George wrote in his diary, 'This is always an ordeal for me & I don't begin to enjoy Christmas until after it is over'.[35] He was much happier when asked to tour the country or visit troops abroad. In November 1941 he arrived in Coventry very soon after that town had been bombed. In June 1943 he was in North Africa and from there he went on to visit the recently besieged island of Malta. Again, ten days after the Allied invasion of Europe, he visited the Normandy beachhead. Even the princesses played their part, and in October 1940 Princess Elizabeth, then aged fourteen, broadcast on the popular radio programme 'Children's Hour', speaking especially to the young people who had been evacuated to the United States and the Dominions. But perhaps the death of the King's younger brother the Duke of Kent in 1942, killed in a flying accident while on active service, did most to remind the country that the Royal Family was also involved in the war. According to a Mass-Observation report, his death did 'more for the popularity of the Royal Family than any other single event could have done'. Sympathy was extended to the Duchess of Kent – 'It's awfully sad, and the baby only 8 weeks old. I

'Somewhere in Holland', George visits No.39 Wing of the Royal Canadian Air Force.

feel very sorry for her… ' – and more general and complimentary remarks were made about the Royal Family as a whole. 'There's nothing one can say about the Royal Family except good – they're homely and simple people and their kindliness and friendliness is an example for us all'.[36]

Overseas, and especially in the United States, the Royal Family was greatly admired. Queen Elizabeth, in particular, had been an outstanding success during the royal tour of the States in 1939, where she had been voted 'Woman of the Year'. Later, during the war, the *New York Herald Tribune* at one point described the royal couple as the 'Ministers of Morale'.[37] In the circumstances of wartime especially, Churchill's remark although cynical was extremely appropriate: 'No institution pays such dividends as the monarchy'.[38] Nevertheless, it would be wrong to conclude; that the attempt to present the Royal Family as the symbol of unity and strength was uniformly successful. Newsreel coverage during the 'phoney war', rather than enhancing the prestige of the monarchy, led, if we are to believe a Mass-Observation report, to a slight but distinct decline in their popularity. Just as other leaders were tending to be discredited during this period of apparent marking-time, so cinema-goers were becoming bored with newsreel items on the Royal Family. 'They are always seen visiting factories, civic centres, or the King on his own awarding medals. Every sequence is similar to the last'. The newsreel companies may well have paid heed to this information and British Movietone News ran far fewer items on the Royal Family over the following two years. Also, towards the end of the war, Mass-Observation were reporting a sizeable percentage of people who felt, if not hostile towards the monarchy, at least indifferent to it.[39]

This reaction was perhaps part of the general disillusionment which developed, as the war progressed, with a number of existing institutions as well as politicians. Nevertheless, Churchill was not simply being gallant when he wrote to the King in 1941, 'This war has drawn the Throne and the people more closely together than ever before recorded, and Your Majesties are more beloved by all classes and conditions than any princes of the past'. George, for his part, came to admire and respect his Prime Minister and 'thought the people were very ungrateful' when Churchill was defeated in the General Election of 1945.[40] Essentially George was a conservative gentleman who did not relish change. He had been sorry to see Chamberlain go in 1940 and would have preferred the more 'solid' Lord Halifax as his successor to the charismatic Churchill. Nevertheless, faced in 1945 with a Labour Government pledged to sweeping changes at home and decolonization abroad, he determined to remain above politics. Although he did not always feel at ease or in agreement with Clement Attlee, he carried out his state duties both in Britain and the Commonwealth as conscientiously as ever. Also, unlike previous monarchs, he was extremely concerned that his eldest daughter should be thoroughly grounded in her future duties. Indeed, as the King's health declined, so the spotlight shifted to Elizabeth. Her marriage to Philip in November 1947 was a glittering state spectacle which came as a relief at a time of deep austerity, and in 1949 Elizabeth attracted the close attention of the media when for the first time she took the salute at the Trooping of the Colour.

George was only fifty-six when he died in February 1952. His wife was convinced that had he remained merely Duke of York he would have lived much longer, and constantly referred to the Duchess of Windsor as 'the woman who killed my husband'.[41] George had worked very hard as King, especially in ensuring that the prestige of the monarchy remained high. In this respect, like his father, he believed in maintaining ceremonials and constitutional proprieties, but he was prepared to adjust to the times, as is best seen in his role as father and family man. In fact, he walked a tightrope, on the one hand ensuring that his family appeared as popular and acceptable figures, but on the other working to preserve the mystique of the monarchy which Bagehot had claimed was so essential. Compared with their counterparts in the Netherlands and Scandinavia, the British Royal Family retained a much greater degree of glamour and formality in the years following the Second World War. The royal presence could still make occasions memorable. The Festival of Britain, for example, seemed doomed to become a damp squib until March 1950 when the King and Queen agreed to become patrons;[42] when the Royal Family drove from Buckingham Palace to open it the following year, the streets were crowded with people wishing to be part of the spectacle.

Had he lived longer George VI might well have found the 1950s uncongenial to his views and his style of kingship. This was to be a decade of rapid social change in which a new prosperity mingled with a certain impatience of established conventions. The age of television was just beginning and marked changes were occurring in the media, especially within the popular press. The days of 'gentlemen's agreements' were passing and the revelations of royal servants fast approaching.

8 Elizabeth II

From Accession to Silver Jubilee

The British monarchy, like the nation it ruled over, retained on the accession of Queen Elizabeth II much of the style and fabric of the early twentieth century. King Edward VIII may have brusquely brought to an end 'Sandringham Time' (the custom by which the clocks at Sandringham House were set half an hour early to ensure a prompt start for shooting parties) on the night of George V's death but, in a deeper sense, Sandringham time still held sway. The impact of the brief reign of Edward, with its mid-Atlantic tone and the aeroplanes, cocktail parties and golf which gave it a flimsy modernity, had been slight. The recovery of the monarchy after the Abdication crisis was based on a return to that combination of majesty and domesticity favoured by George V.

The public and ceremonial face of the institution bore the stamp of an even earlier reign. Royal display and ritual had been burnished and stage set by Edward VII and Viscount Esher and needed little improvement, far less modernization. The 'horse' side of monarchy which the public saw at great ceremonial occasions, at coronations, funerals, military parades and state visits, had reached its apogee as the age of the horse was passing and had, by virtue of conscious anachronism, become even more important and compelling with that passing. The degree of pomp, circumstance and costume that a particular occasion warranted had become governed by traditions that depended on rules, and a calendar for ceremonial monarchy had been set. If neither George V nor George VI had quite the zest for such ceremony as Edward VII, they had greater reverence and played their roles with dignity and punctiliousness.

The more personal social calendar of the Royal Family, the peregrinations to Windsor, Balmoral and Sandringham and the visit to Cowes for the Regatta, followed an Edwardian pattern modified by George V; the long sojourns in European resorts by the 'uncle of Europe' were however omitted and the formality of royal households encased a domesticity that was both proper and cosy. But George VI and his consort presided over a family life which was incomparably more relaxed, spontaneous and British than that of George V and Queen Mary. Among the many benefits which Elizabeth Bowes-Lyon brought to the Royal Family and the monarchy was her completion of the process of anglicizing them. For all George V's oft-proclaimed Englishness or Britishness, his domestic life had been more akin, with its formal cosiness, to that of some German royal family of the late nineteenth century than to the domestic lives of the British aristocracy. George VI's own inclinations and his wife's background created a domestic atmosphere which, though necessarily formal, was closer to the lives of the more solid and tweedy and less fashionable sections of the aristocracy, the sort of people who were their principal courtiers and friends.

A majestic but domestic monarchy had been able to surmount the Abdication crisis and to preserve a cloistered and traditional court, while making cautious use of the mass media. If the monarchy had become a little dowdy and austere during the War and the immediate

Prams fit for a Princess

PEDIGREE present a magnificent new pram—the PRESTIGE.

Beautifully designed and finished, this new PRESTIGE is lovely to look at, lovely to be seen with. And it is presented at such a very reasonable price²—(£15.12.6). See the new PRESTIGE now at any Pedigree Stockist.

All the best babies have a Pedigree

REGD. TRADE MARK

Safety : Notice the special non-tipping device—Exclusive to Pedigree

This advertisement from 1952 shows the continuing attempts to reap profit from association with the monarchy. While you cannot use the Royal Family to advertise a product these days, there is nothing to stop you finding a model with a slight resemblance to a royal mother and a baby who could pass for a two-year-old Princess Anne!

post-war years, and its fabric somewhat frayed and faded, then this, no doubt, suited the national mood and matched the experience of the nation. These had not been years for too much glitter or for a new royal yacht. The people did not grudge the Royal Family their palaces but they did not want them to appear too comfortable in them either; they did not wish them to take to public transport or bicycles, for they liked them to retain some majesty and grandeur, but they relished satisfying fictions such as the news that Princess Elizabeth had to take clothing coupons into account when making her wedding preparations.

By the time of Elizabeth's accession in 1952, however, the nation was tired of austerity. The British people, partly because they overestimated Britain's role in the Allied victory in World War II and thus British strength at the moment of triumph, felt cheated by its drab aftermath and the fall in prestige abroad. The new reign was seen by the media, and doubtless by millions, not only as continuing a much-needed tradition at a time of national decline but also as inaugurating a new era in which prestige and power would be regained and austerity left behind. Perhaps the now distant victory would at last bring some reward.

That the new monarch was both a queen and young inevitably raised comparisons with the great queens of British history, Elizabeth I and Victoria. The notion of a second Elizabethan Age was popular and magazine writers scratched their heads in a desperate search for contemporary equivalents of Drake, Raleigh, and Shakespeare. Some looked back less far. Churchill declared, 'I whose youth was passed in the august, unchallenged and tranquil glare of the Victorian era, may well feel a thrill in invoking once more the prayer and anthem "God Save the Queen"'.[1]

It was, perhaps, a measure of Churchill's Victorian origins that he at first opposed the televising of the Coronation. The growing number of cumbersome television aerials that were spreading across the country were to enable millions of subjects to witness the

Coronation street party, Southsea. The coronation mugs from which the children are drinking have, in the twentieth century, become a feature of the celebrations, often being given away by schools.

ceremony and were to be the major means by which royalty would project itself in the new reign. The large parties which assembled on 2 June 1953 in the homes of those who did possess television sets, for the moment still a minority, far outnumbered the few thousand gathered in the Abbey and the many thousands who lined the streets outside; they in turn were outnumbered by the estimated three hundred million viewers abroad who, thanks to film flown out by specially chartered aircraft, would see the Coronation before the end of the day.

The televising of the Coronation pointed towards a more public monarchy, with almost the entire population witnessing the ritual crowning of their Queen, an event which in the past had been seen only by the highest in the land. The ceremony itself reinforced many traditional aspects of the British monarchy and British society which the post-war years had tended to obscure. It had been conventional in the nineteenth century to remark on the interdependence of monarchy and aristocracy, but by the mid-twentieth century it had become almost equally conventional to play down the links between the two; monarchy had many defenders in 1953, the peerage few. Yet the personal links between the Royal Family and the British aristocracy had grown closer in the twentieth century, even as the grandeur of noble establishments had diminished, while at the same time the need for a peerage as a supporting cast had become more urgent. At the coronations of Edward VII and George V there had been rows of foreign princes, but by 1953 their ranks had long been thinned, while the Commonwealth heads of state did not match the imperial satraps who had attended George VI's coronation. One of the distinguishing features of the British monarchy which sets it apart from modern Continental monarchies is that it sits at the apex of a peerage whose titles have still a legal and constitutional authority. It was the lords temporal and spiritual who made up the main supporting cast at the Coronation and, though some of their robes might be moth-eaten, few would deny that their presence was more appropriate and colourful than serried ranks of Members of Parliament, civic dignitaries and trades union officials would have been.

But the Coronation was more than just a colourful and antique ceremony brilliantly presented, bringing pomp and pageantry into a grey world. Contemporary observers were united in detecting a people re-affirming their faith and pride in themselves, their past and their future. The sociologists Edward Shils and Michael Young saw it as a 'great act of national communion',[2] while Dermot Morrah, looking back on the great occasion, wrote:

> As the great and solemn rites took their stately course, and for the first time were made visible to the multitudes by the new miracle of television, the whole nation felt itself to be rededicated in the person of the Queen. Of the millions throughout the world-wide Commonwealth who were elated by that great uplifting of the heart, there were probably few to reflect that they were repeating the experience of their earliest Christian ancestors; but there is evidence that, in the centuries when the pagan tribes who had swept over the Roman Empire were being converted to the Christian faith, it was usual for the King to be baptised on behalf of all his people, and that out of that mystical representation the later ritual of coronation arose.[3]

Such musings were, no doubt, a little overblown and fanciful but there was truth in their assertion that monarchy, denuded of much of the substance of political power, had retained some of its original spiritual and magical sway, the hopes and beliefs of the people, their very identity, could still be vested in the semi-sacerdotal royal person.

No doubt a young king would have been enthusiastically received by his people, but equally clearly the sex of the new monarch had a lot to do with the mystique of the day: much of the peculiar drama and pathos of the Coronation were derived from the spectacle of the slender female figure at the centre of the solemn ritual. The British, it has been said, are a matriarchal people and certainly no king is so hallowed in the national memory as are Elizabeth I and Victoria. John Pearson has detected an overriding female element in the monarchy from Queen Victoria onwards and has argued that 'under the influence of the Windsor matriarchs, the public image of the British royal males had developed round the dedicated undemanding figures of those family loving kings George V and George VI'.[4] In his thesis, the key figures become Queen Mary and her successor Queen Elizabeth, the Queen Mother, who are seen as the guardians of the sacred kingship. Whether or not a Queen is the monarch, the matriarchy reigns and must be on its guard against wayward or assertive males, who may imperil the institution. Now a Queen was once more on the throne, at once an assurance of constitutional propriety and an inspiration for national recovery.

Inevitably, after so much spiritual and patriotic exaltation, there was a hangover. The Coronation had been a great success and the news on its eve, that a British expedition had conquered Everest, seemed to give credence to the notion of a new Elizabethan Age. But too much confidence and hope had been invested and the Queen could also become the focus of disappointment. The new age had its points – greater prosperity more widely spread, with more television sets and family cars – but national decline continued and the Commonwealth idea that had appealed to Morrah proved a chimera. What was the correct day-to-day role and style for a constitutional monarch whose reign had begun amidst so much emotion? To the Queen and her mother who had, unusually for a dowager queen, taken the title 'Queen Elizabeth, the Queen Mother' to distinguish her from her daughter, there was no problem. The monarchy should proceed in the general manner and with the same style as during the reign of George VI. The Queen's first duty was to remain loyal to the tradition of the father she had been so close to, and to safeguard his inheritance. She had the duties of a constitutional monarch to perform: to be informed and consulted by her government, to take the leading role in state ceremonials, to patronize key institutions and good causes, and to make visits to towns and cities within her realm and to her realms overseas. Otherwise a private life could be led behind the walls of palace and country house, a family brought up and an heir to the throne prepared for his eventual duties. The Queen Mother had skilfully pioneered a discreet method of making vignettes of domestic life and the occasional photo-opportunity available to the press. It was true that the press was becoming restless and more intrusive, and the publication of memoirs by the former governess Miss Marion Crawford ('Crawfie') was a worrying development, but this was not yet a major problem.

By the late 1950s, however, a widespread disenchantment with the failure of the new Elizabethan age to arrest national decline had resulted in an analysis, among those who liked to consider themselves as 'opinion-formers', that the root cause lay in the traditional and ossified nature of British institutions and their domination by the upper and upper-middle classes. A quarry called the 'Establishment' was identified, and unsurprisingly the monarch was seen as setting the tone and style for this network of the high and mighty.[5] In 1957 a series of attacks by republicans and criticisms by radicals and Tory reformers, such as had not been seen since the 1870s, were given considerable publicity. John Osborne thought the monarchy 'a gold filling in a mouth full of decay' but more worrying for the institution were the criticisms of Lord Altrincham and Malcolm Muggeridge, which concentrated upon the royal lifestyle, the way in which the Queen was presented and the quality of her advisers.[6] The gist of the criticisms was that the monarchy was out of touch with contemporary Britain: it was old-fashioned, with a style redolent of the days of the Empire; the Queen sounded upper class or priggish; and the Court was aristocratic and 'tweedy' – the sight of tweeds seemed to induce the same response in journalists that low-flying game birds reputedly had on the tweedy! But it would have been difficult to imagine a non-upper-class queen and it was the monarchy's business to be old-fashioned. Robert Lacey summarized the whole episode well:

> In retrospect the most striking thing about the criticisms of Altrincham, Osborne and Muggeridge was their irrelevance to the Britain of 'I'm all right Jack' and 'Never had it so good'. This obsession with the royal family was, in many ways, as unbalanced as that of the most bedazzled Crawfie addict.[7]

That the monarchy did not lend itself to the craze for a specious and rootless modernity that swept Britain in the fifties and sixties, and withered in the seventies, can be seen in retrospect as wise. There was never much evidence that the wider British public wished the Royal Family to change its style fundamentally. If one strand in the desire to refashion, modernize, merge and streamline the country's institutions and the very physical appearance of its towns and cities was the aim of achieving greater efficiency, another was a distaste and even hatred for the national past on the part of a number of writers, planners and politicians. The monarchy could not lend itself to this latter tendency, for its great strength lay in its maturity and expression of pride in the nation's past achievements. The confident claims that the public desired an end to the vestiges of hierarchy and aristocratic style in public life had to be set against the lack of evidence that Harold Macmillan's 'grouse-moor' image ever did him any real harm with the electorate.

There was some truth in the view that the royal juggernaut needed to update its mode of presentation. No organization, however venerable, be it Buckingham Palace or the Vatican, could thrive in the modern world without efficiency in public relations, Sir Richard Colville, the Queen's Press Secretary until 1968, could not keep the press and television permanently at bay with the methods of the 1930s. The problem was how to modernize the presentation of an institution which gained so much from its traditional and historic nature, without destroying that very nature.

On the whole, the difficulty was dealt with successfully. A new, professional, almost aggressive, approach to publicity was launched in 1968 and 1969 whose architects were William Heseltine, who succeeded Sir Richard Colville, David Checketts, Prince Charles's Equerry and Nigel Neilson of the public relations consultants Neilson McCarthy Ltd.[8] The aims were: to present the informal and domestic side of the Royal Family – after all, it was argued, the public would receive impressions of the private side of royalty from the gossip of courtiers and the breaches of confidence of ex-servants, and it was far better for the royals deliberately to make the impressions they wanted to make; to introduce the adult Prince Charles to the nation as a dignified and hard-working young man; and to make the most of his Investiture as Prince of Wales. They succeeded almost too well. The Investiture itself was the culmination of an exercise in professional presentation, which included the television film *Royal Family*, in which the Queen was seen barbecuing the royal steaks, and a series of interviews on TV and radio in which the Prince talked to such media personalities of the day as Jack de Manio, David Frost and Cliff Michelmore. The Investiture took the monarchy and Royal Family to a new peak of popularity. Undoubtedly there were dangers in the new approach. Having allowed the television cameras into royal sanctums, they could never be kept out again. Did an informal presentation of the Royal Family threaten their position as 'symbols of authority and majesty', as Peregrine Worsthorne suggested? The real danger was the prospect that rather than managing the media, the family would become its quarry. A favourite quarry was to be the Duke of Edinburgh.

The role of husband to the Queen of a matriarchal society is not tailor-made for an energetic and impatient man and it seems clear that Prince Philip has often found his position to be a thankless and frustrating one. The model provided by Prince Albert was not satisfactory, and not just because the position of the monarchy had changed so much

*Engaged in one of her trademark
'walkabouts', the Queen receives a
sticky sweet from a young subject.*

in a hundred years. The Duke of Edinburgh has wisely steered clear of the Queen's political duties, but even the role pioneered by Albert, as patron of the arts and sciences and modernizer of the nation's institutions, was difficult to follow. Since the mid-nineteenth century most of these institutions have expanded considerably, and a prickly, complacent professional defensiveness has grown up around them. Both Prince Philip and his son, Prince Charles, have found that advice to such bodies is rarely welcomed.

Even within the palace walls and in the hierarchy of the Royal Family, Prince Philip's position was not entirely secure. The son of Prince Andrew of Greece and nephew of Earl Mountbatten, Philip had adopted British nationality and his mother's and uncle's name before his marriage to Princess Elizabeth in 1947. The marriage had been zealously promoted by Lord Mountbatten, who combined great wealth (thanks to his marriage), radical views and obsessive pride in his minor royal lineage. His career had been outstanding: naval 'Supremo' in South-East Asia and last Viceroy of India. The seemingly effortless rise of Mountbatten – which, in fact, owed much to a ruthless utilization of his royal connections – had involved a hasty leap from the sinking ship of Edward VIII to the new flagship of George VI. His once close association with the vilified Duke of Windsor had not been forgotten by the Queen Mother, who saw the Mountbattens as a threat to the traditions of the House of Windsor. In this respect, the thinly concealed dispute over the name of the dynasty after the Queen's accession is instructive. In 1952 the Queen, advised by Churchill, declared the continuation of the House of Windsor, thus depriving her descendants of the right to bear the name of Mountbatten. This decision, later modified by a declaration of 1962 which decided that Mountbatten-Windsor would be the family name (though it was not to be used by the immediate royal family[9]), could be defended in light of the fact that 'Windsor' had been specifically invented to stress the British nature of the royal family; but it has been widely interpreted as a triumph for the Queen Mother and court conservatism and as a rebuff for the Mountbattens.

The Queen Mother, as well as being the most consistently popular member of the Royal Family, is a person who combines sweetness and charm with steel and intransigence.[10] She has worked hard to buttress and conserve the institution, and her judgement that the monarchy risks more by bending to the transient whims of modernity than by seeming to be stuffy or old-fashioned is almost certainly correct. The idea, proposed by Philip, of razing Sandringham House and replacing it with a new building representative of modern British architecture, was in keeping with the modernizing spirit of the late 1950s. Today few would regret that the Queen Mother's veto prevailed, the house was refurbished rather than rebuilt, and Sandringham time continued. She, herself, probably still lives in Sandringham time, though to older subjects she seems forever in 'Blitz time', but it is a tribute to her command of her projection of herself that there has been no demand for her 'modernization'.

Prince Philip's dilemmas, in his search for a dignified and purposeful place in national life, are to a considerable extent the problems of all royal males. They have access to a platform from which they can speak about almost everything. Yet they are considered bland and uninspiring when circumspect in their comments, and are bound to upset some lobby or interest if they speak their minds. Throughout their lives they are watched by the baleful eyes of special interest groups, cranks and fanatics of one sort or another. An injudicious cherry brandy drunk by a schoolboy prince captures the headlines; royal shooting parties outrage the herbivorous; foxhunting makes the animal protectionists give voice; while a moment's tardiness in putting on a seat belt activates the pens of road-safety experts. Female royals may not all take pleasure in a career of gracious civility and the patronage of charities and good causes, but the career is not perceived as undignified. Until the 'eighties it was largely by working within a traditional image of womanhood that the Windsor women enjoyed success, and those, like Princess Margaret and Princess Anne who, in their different ways, did not conform to such an image, had a more difficult time of it. Like the royal males they were and are expected to conform to everybody's 'do not'. Princess Margaret, the only public smoker in a family which has included such enthusiasts for the weed as the last four kings, is perpetually advised and nagged to give up and set a good example. Let Princess Anne but chastise a horse or tongue-lash a photographer and she departed from the stereotype of a Princess Royal.

At regular intervals over the last two centuries, the question of the cost of the monarchy has been raised. George III had, as we have seen, queered the royal financial pitch by accepting a much less advantageous arrangement for his Civil List than had been secured by his predecessors. Parliament failed to return his generosity and proved less than enthusiastic in providing dowries and settlements for his children, while in the twentieth century the comparatively modest sums required to maintain the royal establishments proved an easy way to raise a populist outcry.

The late sixties and the seventies were a period of inflation, and despite the general popularity of the monarchy, the royal finances continued to be a headache. The monarchy, announced Prince Philip in 1969, would be 'in the red' by 1970; the Civil List granted on the Queen's accession had, inevitably, made insufficient provision for inflation. There followed a period in which expenditure upon the monarchy and Royal Family loomed larger in the national consciousness than was comfortable for the monarchy. A Select Committee of 1971 looked not only at the Civil List, which in fact accounted for only a small amount of the expenditure, but also at the roles of the various government departments which underwrote the costs of royal palaces and of such items as royal trains, the royal yacht and the Queen's Flight. If the full picture never did emerge this was both because the private financial position of the Royal Family was not divulged and because it proved, in any case, impossible to draw a sharp line between many of the Queen's private possessions and public property. The financial adjustment of 1971 not only provided for a satisfactory increase in the Civil List but in general established a clearer accounting framework for royal expenditure. When the frenetic inflation of the early seventies made these financial provisions inadequate within a few years, the Labour Government took steps designed to remove the entire question from future controversy by providing in 1975 for the royal finances to be regularly updated, in line with inflation.

The episode proved embarrassing to the Royal Family. Although overt republicanism in the House of Commons was largely confined to the one-man band of Mr Willie Hamilton, the cause of increasing the royal purse was not close to the hearts of many Labour backbenchers and, in 1975, ninety MPs voted against the government's proposal. The specific payments made to working royals, those engaged in representative work, continued to be occasionally controversial: they were used as a stick with which to beat those royals who become unpopular or who were perceived as 'not doing their job', by fulfilling an insufficient number of engagements. Minor royals, whether or not they get support from the public purse, may not be particularly well off, but it is very difficult for them to pursue any career besides that of being a member of the royal family; the entrepreneurial activities of Princess Michael of Kent were not met with universal admiration and neither have the recent endeavours of Prince Edward.

It is perhaps only one of the many paradoxes of public opinion that many people demand reductions in the monarchy's income and are nevertheless affronted if a royal female attends a function in a dress that has been seen before, feeling that the British monarchy should still represent the country in style. As a further indignity the Queen, in the early 1990s, was to bow to pressure to pay income tax, ostensibly to herself.

Despite such problems, the reign of Queen Elizabeth could until the 1980s be accounted a quiet success. No great constitutional issues had necessitated the use of the remaining royal prerogatives, though the then structure of the Conservative Party had meant that she had to choose two prime ministers in 1957 and 1963 and her representative, the Governor general of Australia had dismissed a prime minister in 1975.

In 1974 the indefinite result of the general election made it seem for a time that she would have to exercise the crown's prerogatives as to the formation or dismissal of governments. As the Jubilee celebrations of 1977 were to demonstrate the crown was held in restrained but profound affection. The royal family had its domestic problems to be sure but when had this not been the case. The monarchy is generally wise to be a little but not too much behind the times but over the question of divorce it lagged for some time behind society's changing mores. There was wide-spread sympathy for Princess Margaret in the early fifties, when, under pressure, she decided not to marry the divorced man she was in love with. Her divorce from Lord Snowden in the more tolerant seventies proved uncontroversial, though her affair with Roderic Llewellyn cost her much of her erstwhile popularity. The Princess was, however, only fifth in line to the throne at the time. If the personal lives of members of the royal family occasioned considerable press interest in the first decades of the Queen's reign, few could have foreseen the interest that they would be arousde in the eighties and nineties.

The phrase 'the royal soap opera' appears to have been invented by Malcolm Muggeridge. It is a phrase that has become more apposite over time, for both the royal family and soap operas have changed since 1957. In parallel with *Dallas* and *Dynasty*, the marriages of the Prince of Wales and the Duke of York confirmed the notion of a royal soap opera in which the nation can find reflected its fantasies and through which it can follow the fortunes of its favourite and least-favoured characters. Even though the term is less than respectful, it is little more than a modern expression of the fact that since the eighteenth century the public have followed with fascination the developing saga of the Royal Family. They have done so with reverence, deference and adulation but also with prurience, malice and spite. Mass literacy and the mass media have facilitated and fanned the process, but from the days of Rowlandson to *Spitting Image*, and from Greville to the publication of the Windsor love letters, there has been an enormous audience for squibs and gossip concerning the Royal Family. In the eighties, however, with a press armed with telephoto lenses and eavesdropping devices and a public convinced that couples should be either happy or divorced, the soap opera was to have momentous consequences for the monarchy.

9 Adulation and Obloquy
The rise and fall of the glamour monarchy

A perusal of press reports of the Silver Jubilee of 1977 not only confirms the degree to which loyalty to the monarchy was unquestioned in British society but the way in which the celebrations affirmed the nation's continued self-regard. Fêtes and concerts in village halls, far more than processions and formal ceremonies, testified to the continuity of society and culture despite the supposed fundamental changes that sociologists and historians have claimed overtook Britain from the late 'fifties. A drive through country villages on the morning of the day of the Jubilee would have revealed tractor-drawn floats being prepared for local festivities and village greens bedecked with flags, while in towns and cities larger scale events were being prepared and Territorial Regiments, the British Legion, scouts and guides formed up ready to parade to church or town hall. Here were the small platoons that made up the fabric of civil society.

The strength of this expression of public feeling lay in its spontaneous, widespread and restrained nature. There was little that was feverish or frenetic about the celebrations. They just seemed natural. The Queen had reigned for twenty-five years, was well-loved but not adulated and, without much prompting, parish councils, town halls and civil society moved into action and did what they had always done on such occasions, seeing the life-cycle of monarchy as an occasion for affirming what local communities were, as well as declaring loyalty to the crown, which was the ultimate expression, far more than government, of themselves.

How much did it mean? Did it suggest that despite all the changes in society and even of the landscape, despite the 'sixties and the incessant demands for modernization and impatience with established institutions, a 'deep England', even a 'deep Britain', endured? Was it, alternatively, the loyal celebrations themselves that were superficial, a space for nostalgia, for pretending that an older social fabric was still intact and old loyalties maintained and the real world of property speculation, advertising and pop stars was set aside for the day? The Jubilee came, of course, at a time of crisis for the post-war consensus. Keynesian economics and acceptance of the paternalist role of the welfare state had co-existed uneasily for decades with the dynamics of capitalism and the goals of personal enrichment and individual upward mobility, but the contradictions were increasingly obvious and a time for decision arriving. The degree to which the semi-socialism of the post-war Labour governments, the half-hearted free market policies of their Conservative successors, the flimsy modernizations of Wilson and the Janus faces of the Heath administration had left the social and political structures of British society unchanged has been too little remarked upon. Industrialists, county gentry, trades union officials and labour councillors co-existed, not unhappily, within a broad consensus and a general contentment with the constitution, and its apex, the crown, reflected this, Within town and county councils, a place and a leverage on patronage was reserved for both the supposed opposing factions, who were, in fact, happy enough with the compromise. Economic pressures and the failure of British industry brought an end to this.

What is striking about the problems that were to trouble the monarchy after 1977 is not their novelty but the fact that they were the recurrent difficulties that the monarchy had faced during the period covered by this book. Since the reign of George III, the monarchy has regularly had to cope with problems posed by errant royal males and straying princesses and there have been furores in many reigns over royal finances. The marriages and sex lives of members of the royal family are part of the institution of monarchy for, if the marital circumstances of presidents or prime ministers, their well-publicized domestic bliss or their exposed sexual transgressions, arouse interest, admiration or criticism, they are not intrinsic to the office and are, in any case, as ephemeral as the tenure of elected office itself. For a hereditary dynasty, living out life cycles almost on behalf of the nation, what little distinction there had ever been between public and private life was rapidly eroded by the intrusions of the press. If the essential problems of the monarchy were age old, they were placed in a new context by the ubiquity and arrogance of the media and by changing social mores. Few in the thirties had had any idea about the Duke of Kent's drug-taking or of the affairs of Princess Marina and Edwina Mountbatten thanks to the discretion of the press. Prince Charles, Princess Diana and the Duchess of York were not to benefit from a similar discretion. Now the media was not only to take delight in reporting the occasional Alf Garnett type xenophobic remarks of Prince Philip but enthusiastically set itself the task of unearthing as many intimate stories and pictures, especially of the younger members of the royal family, as possible.

Even without major scandals, the presentation of the monarchy and the royal family would have posed problems. The aim of the palace was, of course, to keep control, to use the media to protect the royal family, rather than allow the media to intrude upon the family. The loyalty and discretion of the press had meant that the Abdication crisis had only been a crisis so far as the wider public was concerned for a matter of weeks, while skilful use of newspapers and newsreels had helped establish a positive image of George VI and his family as dignified yet, withal, an ordinary loving family. The contemporary press could, it was hoped be used in a similar way. Such hopes were optimistic.

The question of the presentation of monarchy in a society with a seemingly insatiable appetite for information about the royal family and the technical ability to transmit such information instantly to millions turned public relations into an almost permanent royal preoccupation. What the royal advisers did not appreciate was the way society and journalism were changing. The circumspection with which the media had treated the monarchy had by the late sixties become more a matter of habit than a policy. Both deference and respect for privacy were rapidly breaking down, while a taste for sensation and scandal, traditionally characteristic of a couple of Sunday newspapers, was spreading to the respectable broadsheets. The public had 'a right to know', a right to know everything. Heroes and heroines were made and cherished by the media, footballers, pop stars, entrepreneurs *et al*, but the media made them kings for a day before delighting in their fall, when their drug habits, their sex lives or their sharp business practices were exposed. At least they enjoyed a brief acclaim in contrast to the representatives of tradition. There were no prizes for the investigative journalist or television producer who found the establishment sound or an old institution still doing a fine job. The palace shortened the spoon with which it supped in such company at its peril. The relationship of the monarchy and the media was to progressively deteriorate and what began amidst the serenity of a stage-managed barbecue was to lead to the intrusions of the *paparazzi*, bugged palaces and intercepted phone calls. It was as if the producers of a rather sedate television series, a long-running family saga, had suddenly decided to modernize it and make it more sensational; the scriptwriters then went mad and the producers lost control.

The attitudes and character of the media can be seen as either subversive of society's mores or as reflecting them. Both views are probably naïve. A newspaper depending upon purchasers or a television station which stands or falls on its viewing figures cannot afford to offend too many readers or viewers. The media is, nevertheless, influential when it probes across the boundaries of yesterday's good taste and questions respect for the established order and values, provided it has accurately diagnosed the numbers it can carry with it or, most importantly, judged accurately the prevailing correctness of the real establishment. The media's intrusion into the private lives of the royal family, though to some extent invited, was only an aspect of the intrusion into the private lives of anyone who was powerful or famous and reflected a major change in society. Essentially society became more meritocratic, more individualist and more materialist; the social structure changed and the old class structure seemed redundant, while mobility, both geographical and social, increased. However economically dynamic the new order of the 1980s was, there can be no doubt that it fractured much of the hitherto prevailing social order. While it increased material inequality, it destroyed the social hierarchy. This did not diminish but rather increased envy, while economic utility became the yardstick. This was a difficult climate for monarchy, dependent upon respect for tradition, social unity and the composite of integral localities and national identity.

The problems of the monarchy, though it made its own mistakes, were in general the problems of the nation. What was demanded of the monarchy? There was a vague feeling it should be seen to be more 'modern'. No one was quite sure what form this more modern monarchy should take. 'More informal' was a popular interpretation. A Scandinavian or Dutch model was often discussed, for there was a hazy image of bicycling, bus-catching and shopping-basket-carrying royals, which didn't bare much resemblance to any actual European royal family. The populist demand that the monarchy should be less redolent of country houses and less associated with the traditional upper classes was unrealistic. Certain traditions such as the presentation of debutantes at court had already been done away with but did the nation really want a suburban monarchy and was a classless monarchy possible save by royalty going back to being a class of its own? The monarchy had, of course, evolved during the century. It had become more British and it *had* become more informal. The marriage of George VI and Queen Elizabeth, a marriage between a prince and a commoner, following on from the launch of the House of Windsor and more distant relations with the German royal cousinhood, had made the monarchy much more British. No member of the royal family had been more informal than Edward VIII but that was not a happy precedent. Queen Elizabeth and Prince Philip had broken with tradition by sending their children to public schools where they had mixed with a far wider section of the upper classes on more or less equal terms than previous generations.

Andrew Morton has referred to the Queen's children as a 'hybrid generation, enjoying a taste of freedom but anchored to the world of castles and royal protocol'[1] but it is difficult to see how there could be much more freedom given with not only the need for detective escorts but the constant presence of those less welcome escorts, photographers and journalists. Indeed Princes Charles, Andrew and Edward and Princess Anne probably enjoyed less freedom than had their grandparents' generation, much of whose social life went unreported.

As ever, the main question was the upbringing of the heir to the throne, when and whom he should marry and what his responsibilities should be during what promised to be a long apprenticeship. The deliberations over Prince Charles's upbringing were haunted not just by the ghosts of previous male heirs but by the living example of the Queen's Uncle David, for twenty-five years Prince of Wales and for one year King. The plans for Charles's education, as for former heirs apparent, were determined as much by what he should not be and whom he should not be like as by a positive model. As with George IV, Edward VII and Edward VIII, the route mapped out for Prince Charles was carefully worked out, but left little room for flexible modification as the boy's character, strengths, weaknesses and sensitivities were revealed. Prince Philip is not a particularly sensitive man, and he had clear views as to his eldest son's education. The dynasty's traditional problem of the relationship between incumbents and heirs was to be demonstrated once more. If Gordonstoun School, with its mixture of Spartan lifestyle and Platonic ethos, seemed appropriate and even an adventurous choice to Prince Philip, who was an old boy, it was clearly wildly unsuitable for the rather diffident Prince Charles. Eton would have provided a more relaxed atmosphere and almost certainly enabled him to develop his academic interests more fully.

An awful lot was demanded of him and he responded dutifully. As he grew older his education was constantly interrupted by the demands of royal duties or sidetracked by the needs of public relations. The Commonwealth dimension of the monarchy led to his spending six months in Australia at Geelong Grammar School's annexe in the outback, a valuable experience which he enjoyed but which necessarily meant a break from his A-level studies. The perceived need for a Prince of Wales to know some Welsh at a time of quickening Welsh nationalism took him from Cambridge to Aberystwyth for a term. This enabled him to make part of his speech in competent Welsh at his investiture as Prince of Wales at Caernarvon Castle but must have been a distraction from his Cambridge studies. Even when he followed tradition and joined the armed forces, he spent some time in the RAF, taking the graduate course at Cranwell in five months instead of the usual year, before going on to Dartmouth and the Royal Navy. It might have been easier had there been two Prince Charleses. Everything was subordinated to the training of a future king but, when he left the Royal Navy in 1976, it was not to be a king but to be a full-time heir apparent, the second most important member of the 'family firm'.

Representing his mother and sovereign on visits to Commonwealth and other countries, opening new hospitals and presiding at the annual dinners of innumerable institutions were, no doubt, useful and honourable tasks but was there a role that was other than ceremonial and which could be made personal and distinctive? No previous Prince of Wales had succeeded in finding one. Was Prince Charles condemned to adorn

Prince Charles on royal duties. Walkabouts may be informal and relaxed but note the detective close to Charles at the extreme left of the picture.

the 'dignified' part of the constitution? Clearly he has striven to find an individual role for himself. His support for a range of causes, conservation of the environment, concern for disadvantaged youth and the state of the inner cities and his campaign against much of modern architecture, recall, if any previous prince, Victoria's consort, Prince Albert, rather than any of his predecessors as Prince of Wales.

His marriage was long awaited. No previous Prince of Wales, apart from his Uncle David, had remained a bachelor for so long. This was not an appealing precedent. The Prince's delight in dangerous sports also recalled his uncle's reckless steeplechasing. Charles loved piloting his own aircraft and was an enthusiastic polo player. In 1972 he spun off the track while trying out a Formula II racing car. Clearly, many felt, it was time he settled down. Charles had welcomed Lord Mountbatten's advice to have a number of discrete affairs, though he would almost certainly have done this anyway, but the second part of this great avuncular guidance was to then:

> …choose a suitable, attractive and sweet-charactered girl *before* she has met anyone else she might fall for. After all Mummy never seriously thought of anyone else after the Dartmouth encounter when she was 13! I think it is disturbing for women to have experiences if they have to remain on a pedestal after marriage.[2]

127

This was clearly a case of 'do as I say' rather than 'do as I do' for the model bride scarcely resembled Edwina Mountbatten, but Lord Louis was thinking of the special circumstance of a bride who would be Queen. The question was what sort of young woman a late twentieth century Prince of Wales should marry.

There was the traditional model, which meant scouring the protestant royal houses of Europe for a suitable princess, one who would herself have been brought up for a public role. The marriage of George VI to a commoner, albeit an aristocrat, had, however, been an enormous success and the Queen Mother enjoyed great popularity. Should Charles marry within his own generation or choose a bride who was considerably younger? Here the virginity question raised by Lord Mountbatten came into play. Social mores had changed and there were few thirty-year-old virgins around but could the future king marry a girl who had been to bed with someone else? Charles had by the late 1970s had close relationships with a long list of girls including Lucia Santa Cruz, Lady Jane Wellesley, Davina Sheffield and Lady Camilla Shand. He was somewhat in love with all of them but most deeply with Camilla Shand, great granddaughter of Edward VII's mistress Alice Keppel. For diverse reasons, none of these liaisons ended in marriage: because of religion or on account of a past; because Charles was still enjoying bachelor life and couldn't bring himself to take the plunge; or because his sense of duty propelled him towards a marriage in the interests of the throne rather than his own inclinations.

In the end Lord Mountbatten's advice was followed. Charles's name had been linked with Lady Sarah Spencer, daughter of Earl Spencer who had been an equerry to the Queen, but in 1977 he met her younger sister, then sixteen and at boarding school, Lady Diana Spencer. He married her four years later. Here was what seemed the perfect combination, a virgin bride from an old aristocratic family, close to the court and its ways, yet unstuffy and; like a number of upper-class girls, dubbed Sloane Rangers, living and working, not too seriously, in London. The nation immediately fell in love with her, rather more, so it was to transpire, than had Charles.

The wedding took place on 29 July 1981 and attracted the largest worldwide audience ever: 109 TV companies were involved in transmitting the procession and ceremony to 750 million people in seventy-four countries. Elaborately and skilfully stage-managed, the whole event, from the drive to St Paul's with Diana in a glass coach and Charles in a Landau escorted by the household cavalry, through the service itself, which involved three orchestras, to the appearance on the balcony of Buckingham Palace, was a triumph. Royal weddings had always been popular occasions but this one seemed a national emotional experience.

Diana brought to the monarchy a rather dangerous quality: glamour. Not since Edward VIII was Prince of Wales had there been a royal superstar and Diana shared many qualities with him. She was a face and a figure demanding a photographer, for the camera was not just kind to her but caressed her, enhancing her looks and capturing the combination of natural elegance and vulnerability that has proved the essence of a genre of twentieth century icons such as James Dean or, again, Edward Prince of Wales. From the first famous press picture of the *ingénue* Sloane standing, in a skirt made transparent by the sunshine, outside the nursery school where she worked, her image had no rival when it came to selling a magazine or making clothes, hairstyles, charities or causes fashionable.

The marriage of Charles, Prince of Wales, to the beautiful Lady Diana Spencer attracted the attention of the world's media. Portrait of the Princess of Wales by Bryan Organ.

That there was no great depth and much confusion behind the fascinating smile and physical magnetism is yet another parallel with Edward VIII.

That the Princess's educational background was slight and her mind and opinions unformed may well not have appeared defects to the Prince and the Palace. She was from the right sort of background and would presumably conform to royal ways and fit in with Charles's lifestyle. Dazzled by the Prince's attention, it is perhaps not surprising that Diana aimed to please him, exaggerating her liking for country life and the appeal of long walks and wet labradors, while hanging on the words of her suitor. Had the Palace run a psychological tooth-comb over the Princess's emotional balance and the effects on her of her parents' divorce it would have revealed an emotionally unstable yet manipulative young woman. It has been suggested that both her father and her grandmother, Lady Fermoy, later regretted not revealing Diana's mental condition[3], which has been described as 'borderline personality disorder'.[4] Charles himself, with the feelings of inadequacy he hid behind a formal exterior, his diffident self-importance and resigned dedication to duty, was not able to give such a wife the constant attention she demanded. If Diana brought to her new role her charm, looks and elegance, she lacked the capacity to act in the interests of her position rather than to employ the position to further her own wishes, impulses and fantasies. Few seem to have considered the effect that public adulation and the constant attention of the media might have on a charismatic but not very intelligent young woman, though it is significant that within a few months of the marriage the House of Windsor was anxiously arranging psychiatric care for the Princess.

In the long, drawn-out tragedy of the marriage neither partner behaved well. Diana demanded constant affirmation of her husband's affection, found his seriousness boring, his family unsympathetic and his friends stuffy, while she quickly learned that the admiration of the media and its interest in everything she did, said or wore gave her the attention she craved. Charles found his wife's sulks and tantrums inexplicable and self-indulgent and couldn't understand why she didn't conform to his expectations of her. There were reconciliations and times when things went fairly well, while the birth of Prince William and then Prince Harry brought the couple back together for a time, but by 1985, only a year after Harry's birth, the marriage was all but over against a background of Diana's hysterics, bulimia and suicide attempts and Charles's moroseness. By the time Charles was unfaithful with his old flame, Camilla Shand, now Camilla Parker-Bowles, Diana, though Charles did not know this till later, had already taken a number of lovers.

Few marriages have broken up so publicly. Much of the drama was played out in front of the press, telephone calls were intercepted and assignations spied upon, both partners inspired books and were interviewed on television, while Diana's lovers told their tales. It was an *opera bouffe*, George IV and Caroline with moving pictures and an almost literate mass readership for scandal. In the play for public admiration and sympathy Diana was an easy and inevitable winner, at least with the most vociferous, sentimental and angry sections of society. Charles has a charisma which he can project on small audiences but on a bigger stage he seems awkward and ill at ease, while Diana had her super star appeal and an uncanny ability to perform in public as if in a studio. She was at once glamorous and portrayed as a victim in a society which loved victims, especially if they were photogenic. She quickly learned how to manipulate the press, to feed a story to a favourite journalist or spread it via a confidante. In return the press was indulgent to her, suppressing the details of her private life for many years. Paradoxes abounded: an Armani clad underdog; an aristocratic protagonist for the common woman; Mother Theresa one day, Jerry Hall the next; an ordinary mum on a millionaire's yacht; a woman wronged with a string of lovers; and a modern caring Princess touching the sick like Charles I. She became the focus for those who were discontented and almost any pressure group could imagine her their champion.

The royal soap opera's audience grew daily but not with the stories that the semi-professional royal public relations people had hoped to write. Other royal marriages were going wrong as well. Prince Andrew, Duke of York, an amiable naval officer, had cast aside his first love, the actress Koo Stark, and married Sarah Ferguson, portrayed by the press as feisty and fun-loving, but in fact irresponsible, vulgar and publicity-seeking. If the Charles-Diana marriage had elements of tragedy, the York's was pure farce, a farce played by the Duchess in less than flattering tights. We were back to the Regency but with *paparazzi*. Even Princess Anne's marriage foundered. Of all the royal children, she had inherited her father's character and was intelligent, not very sensitive but dedicated to the causes she adopted. Her marriage to fellow horse enthusiast , Captain Mark Phillips, ended in divorce.

130

Perhaps it was not such a good idea for royalty to marry commoners. As Andrew Morton has written:

> Apart from the marriage of George VI every significant match between royalty and commoner has ended in divorce: Princess Margaret and Anthony Armstrong-Jones, Princess Anne and Captain Mark Phillips, and the Duke and Duchess of York and the Prince and Princess of Wales.[5]

One wonders, however, whether endogamous royal marriages would have fared much better in an age when the establishment's solidarity and the media's respect for privacy are long gone and when a population, increasingly promiscuous itself, leers at every transgression by its rulers. Half a century earlier the couples might have become estranged but remained married while discretely conducting their love affairs protected by a benevolent consensus. Much earlier they would have been lampooned by cartoonists but divorce would have been all but impossible, though George IV did, of course, attempt it. Much of late twentieth-century upper-class society might well have happily connived with unorthodox domestic arrangements but the press, at once prurient and sanctimonious, had its cheque books and it was not only servants who told tales.

Any chances of preserving the formalities of marriage were destroyed for the Prince and Princess of Wales by the exhibitionism of Diana, who co-operated with Andrew Morton on his *Diana, Her True Story*, published in 1992. This signalled the end of the marriage. It was followed by the publication of transcripts of tape-recordings of phone calls between Diana and James Gilby, 'Squidgygate' as the furore became known because of Gilby's affectionate nickname for her. The formal separation of Charles and Diana was announced at the end of the year.

The Queen referred to 1992, the year in which she celebrated forty years on the throne, as the *annus horribilis*, and the fire at Windsor Castle seemed to symbolize the monarchy's problems. Shortly afterwards she and Prince Charles agreed to pay income tax on their private income and the Civil List was reduced by £900,000 and restricted to the Queen, the Queen Mother and the Duke of Edinburgh. The tribulations of the House of Windsor were, however, far from over.

Early in 1993 a further set of tapes, this time of conversations between the Prince and Camilla Parker-Bowles, were published, first in America and then in the British press. 'Sqidgygate' had been snapped by 'Camillagate'. Now it was war. Charles's exasperated but unwise decision to retaliate by co-operating with Jonathan Dimbleby on a TV film and book in which he admitted to his affair with Camilla was followed by one of Diana's great performances when, interviewed on BBC's *Panorama*, she first complained about her treatment by her husband and his affair with Camilla – 'There were three of us in this marriage' – then talked of her affair with Major James Hewitt before going on to profess her wish to be 'a Queen in people's hearts'. Divorce proceedings followed and in August 1996 a decree absolute formally ended the marriage. The Princess was now Diana, Princess of Wales but she was no longer a Royal Highness and, as with the Duchess of Windsor more than half a century previously, the decision to withhold the HRH designation was controversial.

A divorced and bitter Princess of Wales seemed to promise decades in which there would be a loose cannon on the ship of Majesty. Diana was not going to go quietly into discrete retirement. She had experienced the adrenaline of public adulation and she was a star not only in Britain but internationally. Several roles were open to her: she could be the centre of an alternative court, tussling with her ex-husband for the affections of the nation; she could join the ranks of the international rich and famous and make the cover of *Hello* magazine several times a year; or she could concentrate upon good causes and become a standing reproach to governments for their neglect of the ills of the world. In the end, she attempted to combine all these roles and was the 'soccer mum' at the funfair with her sons in baseball caps, one of the *glitterati* at the funeral of Italian fashion designer Versace, and the influential face of the campaign to ban land-mines.

Whether the love affair between Diana and the British public would have lasted is debatable. In an interview with *Le Monde* she expressed her dissatisfaction with Britain, which she said she would already have left were it not for the boys. America seemed increasingly a natural habitat though perhaps she was becoming one of those international personalities who flit from resorts to glittering functions with no permanent national base. The affair with Dodi Fayed, playboy son of Mohammed Al Fayed, a man of dubious background and even more dubious business practices, which she began in the summer of 1987, seemed likely to lower her standing with the British public, a standing already lowered when Julia Carling accused her of having an affair with her husband , rugby player Will Carling. It is probable that the gap between the idealized and the real Diana was becoming evident to all bar the deliberately blind but all was changed by a car-crash in Paris.

That Mohammed al Fayed was the owner of the château of the late Duke and Duchess of Windsor, and that this may well have been the destination of Dodi Fayed and the Princess when they left the Ritz Hotel in Paris points to parallels that the most daring script writer might well eschew. Was it Wallis Simpson or the King for a year himself that Diana most resembled? For the wife of one Prince of Wales to die with her lover on the way to the one-time home of an exiled former Prince of Wales was, at the least, ironic.

Princess Diana's death sent a large section of the British public into an astonishing state of collective hysteria fanned by the feeding frenzy of most of the press. The beatification of Diana took place during an incredible week of public grief that climaxed with her funeral. The monarchy, it was claimed, rocked. The Prime Minister, never at a loss for an apposite sound-bite, bewailed the death of the 'People's Princess', while others repeated Diana's own phrase 'The Queen of Hearts'.

Both the mourning itself and commentary upon it revealed a wealth of contradictions. Diana was hailed as a force for republicanism, yet it was her royal status, however ambivalent, that made her coffin the centre of national theatre. The privileged daughter of an old aristocratic family became the symbol of anti-establishment feeling. She was considered a modern figure in contrast to the old-fashioned ways of the House of Windsor, yet modernity is almost always taken to be a move towards the rational and the secular and there was little of either in the mystical and superstitious atmosphere of the week after her death. One commentator noted the 'quasi-religious view of Diana' but recalled that 'In 1935, 1936, and 1937, years of many royal events, Kingsley Martin, the

Princess Diana's funeral turned into a national outpouring of emotion, with hundreds of thousands of people gathering outside Westminster Abbey and along the entire route of her journey to her family home.

editor of the *New Statesman,* was astonished at the 'recrudescence of sheer superstition' surrounding the monarchy.'[6] Her own beliefs appear to have been an uneasy mixture of the cults of self-fulfilment, therapy and astrology, while the hugs, tears, uninhibited emotional release, the candles and flowers, which characterized the mourning, spoke of a society which had abandoned established religion but not embraced cold reason.

There was, no doubt, another Britain that held itself apart from this mass emotional catharsis, a Britain of much reviled stiff upper lips, puzzled and disturbed by the wobbly lips and the hysteria, but the media did not seek it out. Even normally sensible public figures succumbed to the apparent consensus and many of them may well look back in horror at words they said then. A very genuine wave of grief for the death of the beautiful young woman in which so much hope had been invested sixteen years earlier was surfed by those who sought to make Diana a symbol for their own causes, discontents and unhappiness. As Robert Lacey has written, she was 'embraced by the public for motives that range from collusive fantasy to individual dysfunction. For every bouquet of flowers laid to Diana there is a separate private tale to be told.'[7] Opinion columns thundered and columnists shrieked. Within days of Diana's death instant punditry had laid the ground for canonization and soon the first books appeared. The shrill voice of Julie Burchill was to claim the Princess as a feminist icon 'stalked, trapped, used and abused' by the House of Windsor but forged by the flames of her experience into a scourge of men and especially Englishmen.[8] Beatrice Campbell, clutching her working-class credentials to her feminist bosom, analysed the whole saga in terms of sexual politics, a war between her heroine and an upper-class male establishment.[9] New ageism rubbed shoulders with the mediaeval as fortune-telling mingled with psychotherapy, the cult of the 'royal touch' was revived and an eccentric Marianism beatified a woman who had died with a playboy lover.

The power of the week cannot be denied. It was a mixture of the sublime and the vulgar. The Royal Horse Artillery escorted the coffin to St Paul's where, amidst the high ceremony, a recycled pop song first dedicated to that other twentieth-century superstar, Marilyn Monroe, was sung by its composer, Elton John. In Harrods, temple of consumerism, Mohammed al Fayed erected a monument to his son Dodi and the 'People's Princess'.

Could the monarchy survive? Those who doubted that it could underestimated its underlying strength and the number of those who had not succumbed to the emotional extremes of the time. The moment of high tension passed and some months later seemed unreal. Diana's death marked the peak of public disillusion with the royal family and the cult that threatened to form around her memory withered. Yet there is no doubt that the glamour monarchy inaugurated in 1981 and its subsequent disintegration had gravely harmed the institution. A less confident and somewhat battered monarchy was to tiptoe into the twenty-first century.

Conclusion

The years from the mid-eighties until Diana's death had indeed been soap opera years. The almost perpetual need to deal defensively with the media and react to the next scandal had prevented the Palace and the Prince of Wales's office from publicizing their plans for the development of the monarchy and drawing attention to its many achievements. A further problem had been the lack of co-ordination and a degree of distrust between the secretaries and advisors of the Queen and the Prince. If the dynasty that became the House of Windsor has had one consistent attitude over nearly three centuries, save during Edward VII's reign, it is 'never trust the Prince of Wales'. The years since Charles's marriage had done much to harden this attitude and it was clear that the Queen continued to be uneasy about the Prince's relationship with Camilla Parker-Bowles. It had been the Prince, however, who had realized that the funeral of Diana, Princess of Wales could not be that of an ordinary subject and after that event relations between the Queen's household and the Prince's improved. The royal family was, after all, a family firm.

The last years of the century revealed the strengths of the Prince of Wales as the eighties and most of the nineties had revealed his weaknesses. The trials of his marriage and the criticisms of the press had brought out the worst in him. It was natural that he should have been irritated in the lack of interest shown by reporters in the work of the Prince of Wales's Trust and his successful efforts on behalf of young people and the inner cities in contrast to their obsession with his wife, her clothes and *her* charities, It was understandable that he was disappointed with the reception to his initiatives on the environment, alternative medicine, organic farming and public architecture, though those who launch campaigns must expect brickbats. His reaction appears to have been to become gloomy and increasingly sorry for himself. His travails brought out what a sympathetic biographer has called his 'tendency to whinge'.[1] By the late nineties however his 'green' interests seemed much more in tune with the times, the success of the Trust was widely recognized as using a little money more effectively than government initiatives used a lot of money, while, if his architectural endowments had foundered, his architectural tastes could be seen as in touch with much of the population if not those dominant in the architectural profession. His visit to Omagh after the IRA bomb outrage in August 1998 demonstrated that a royal presence demonstrates the wider care of the nation better than the visits of a host of politicians.

A 'Way Ahead Group' had already been formed on the suggestion of the Duke of Edinburgh but the crisis of 1997 made the joint planning and co-ordination this provided for a matter of urgency. It was not, however, easy to see what the way ahead was. Having ceased to exercise so many of its political prerogatives, there are few functions of the monarchy that can be dropped without destroying the monarchy so changes are limited to matters of style. If the monarchy is a symbol of the nation that reflects an image of the nation then its role is peculiarly difficult when the nation is confused as to its identity. The problems of the monarchy are to a great degree the problems of a confused and divided Britain. Conversely, however, its strength is that is better able than politicians to relate to civil society despite the many fractures in that society.

As society grows richer, both greed and envy seem to increase; great inequity in the distribution of wealth is easily accepted when it comes to footballers, actors or pop stars but social privilege and any link between it and wealth greatly resented. The cost of the monarchy, a contentious issue in the seventies, became once more an issue in the nineties. In 1990 the Conservative government introduced a ten-year system for reviewing the Civil List but other measures of the nineties had the effect of reducing the monarchy's income and of threatening the execution of its duties. One was the voluntary decision of the Queen to pay income tax on the Privy Purse and her personal income while another was the announcement that she would reimburse parliament for the parliamentary annuities paid to meet official expenses for all other members of the royal family except for the Queen Mother and the Duke of Edinburgh.

There are strong pressures for a more compact and less expensive monarchy but giving way to such pressures will probably result in a less effective monarchy and the savings to the taxpayer will be small and may even be counterproductive. The failure to build a new royal yacht is a case in point. It may have saved money in the short term but *Britannia* not only gave *éclat* to royal visits but served as a platform for the promotion of Britain's economic interests. Not only is the cost of maintaining the monarchy in its present style modest enough in terms of gross public expenditure, it is dwarfed by the financial benefits it brings indirectly to British business and directly to tourism. To reduce the active royal family to the Queen, Prince Philip, their children and the children of the Prince of Wales would inevitably reduce the number of public engagements that the family could fulfil. This would weaken the everyday leadership of civil society that is constantly, if quietly, demonstrated by visits to provincial towns and rural areas, when schools, hospitals, businesses and public buildings have their big moments, their new premises or extensions, marked by a royal presence. It would also result in the diminution of what is increasingly recognized as a major role of the modern monarchy, the patronage of charities.

Since the late eighteenth century, royalty and charitable causes have become inseparable. The very ubiquity of the spectacle of members of the royal family opening new hospitals, unveiling plaques to commemorate their inauguration of housing projects or presiding over the annual dinners of charities has disguised its centrality to the strength of the institution of monarchy. Royal charity, as Frank Prochaska has pointed out, has not only been good for charities and given a warm and caring image to the monarchy, it has been an essential force in preserving the cohesion and independence of civil society for by devoting so much time to charitable and social causes the monarchy has penetrated deep into that society. At once the apex of the state, but in ethos rather than practice, and the leader of civil society in its work for the public good, the monarchy protects society from monolithic government and provides a bond between state and people. It is a role which no presidency could emulate, nor indeed some slimmed down monarchy do so well.2 In the end, however, monarchy must have an appeal that goes beyond utilitarianism. It must have its sublime and mystical aspects. It must remind the people who they are. This was easier in 1977 than at the end of the century. Britain changed considerably in the 1980s. Thatcherism is not a totally accurate term with which to describe such changes but it is a useful shorthand. The period saw a distinct swing to free market economics with beneficial effects on national competitiveness and economic growth but its social effects were complex. Though the ostensible targets were trade union power and the interventionist state, the traditional order of society and established institutions were called into question by rapid social mobility and a radical onslaught on all that was not obviously efficient. Social conservatism was as much the victim as quasi-socialism. As the established consensus fell apart, social hierarchy and deference went with it. If the monarchy was not directly threatened, it was left somewhat naked as its buttresses in state and civil society were weakened. Had the monarchy, no less than civil service, the BBC, older universities, aristocracy and civic dignitaries, to justify its utility? The glitter of the royal weddings disguised the extent of the challenge but when the media turned on the monarchy with the failure of the marriages, the monarchy seemed dangerously exposed.

Retreat into a purely dignified role is not an option but neither surely is a populist people's monarchy which would soon exhaust its novelty. The practical work of the monarchy which goes on day by day encouraging and leading the civic and charitable aspects of society, soothing and giving hope to the dispossessed and stimulating business initiatives depends in the end upon the mystique and dignity of the institution The case for greater concentration on the functions of the institution rather than upon the personal lives of the royal family is persuasive but it is the individuals and the passage of generations which reinvigorate or threaten the institution. The very nature of monarchy means that there will be peaks and troughs, times for the celebration of births and marriages as for mourning, acclamations for youth and admiration for serene old age, and times when there are no great events to acclaim or bewail. Its capacity for regeneration is innate and comes with time and new generations. The Queen Mother's ninety-ninth birthday preceded the millennium celebrations and Prince William's eighteenth will follow them. A family on the throne continues to be 'an interesting idea'. The danger is that the family has increasingly to live like one of those families in TV 'fly on the wall' documentaries where cameras are ever present.

The twin challenges to the monarchy are thus how to relate to an increasingly fractured and individualist society and how to survive the constant attention and intrusion of the media. Prince Charles has, sometimes clumsily and occasionally maladroitly, but with steady purpose addressed the former but whether any press code can restrain the media seems doubtful. Despite its problems there seems little evidence that the monarchy is in crisis. As a recent study of the monarchy and the British constitution has argued:

> In general, where republicanism has triumphed, this has been less as a result of conscious and deliberate choice than because the monarchy has been discredited either by defeat in war or by resistance to constitutional change. Republicanism in practice is adopted less because it seems an ideal system than because it is all that is left after monarchy has been rendered unsustainable.3

Prince Charles. As heir apparent it is his challenge to help the monarchy adapt successfully to our changing times.

Enthusiasm for a republic in contemporary Britain is restricted to a small minority though such sentiments are more active among a voluble section of society than they have been since the 1860s. The arguments for a republic are not compelling. It is suggested that the monarchy is incompatible with a 'modern' society or with democracy but it is precisely the existence of the monarchy which has enabled constitutional change to take place so smoothly and peacefully in Britain, while, in general, countries with monarchies are not noted for being less modern than those which are republics. The appeal for mechanistic logic and symmetry in all our institutions will, of course, always be denied by the monarchy but the case that such qualities make for effective institutions is a weak one. Monarchy ensures continuity and legitimacy and opinion polls have demonstrated steady support for it during all the vicissitudes of the last quarter century with between 70 and 80% of the population believing a monarchy to be preferable to a republic.

The great challenge to the monarchy largely reflects the changing position of Britain and the question of British identity. The Queen ascended to the throne only a few years after her father ceased to be Emperor of India and the early years of her reign saw the rapid dissolution of the British Empire. If the great hopes placed in the Commonwealth in the 'fifties have not been fulfilled, she remains head of the Commonwealth and Queen of many of its constituent parts and has very obviously a great affection for it. Such affection has not always been shared by recent British governments. Whether Australia, New Zealand, Canada and the other parts of the Commonwealth which still retain the Queen as their monarch will do so for long in the twenty-first century is much debated, as is whether Prince Charles will succeed her as head of the Commonwealth, though, if he were not to do so, it would destroy the most obvious link between the members of that organization. Perhaps more pressing is the question as to how the monarchy will adapt to Scottish and Welsh devolution. There are many precedents, not least that of the union of the crowns, which existed before the act of union and the present position of the Queen as head of state of Commonwealth countries, for monarchs ruling over multiple kingdoms or federations but the danger exists of the monarchy being largely identified with England. Recent steps, such as the Queen making more use of Holyrood Palace and the build up of the Princess Royal as the member of the family most intimately associated with Scotland, demonstrates that the Palace recognizes this danger.

The British monarchy has exhibited a great capacity for regeneration. If this has involved some conscious reinvention as with the new theatre of monarchy stage-managed by Lord Esher, it has largely been an unplanned process, in part a response to public feeling but due largely to the way each monarch has interpreted his or her role within the mores of the day. It has been suggested that the period of the 'magical ' monarchy may be coming to an end and that a new more practical and secular monarchy is required. A society which has become more secular may, however, have simply found new superstitions with which to replace religion as the feverish and evanescent popularity of the glamour monarchy revealed, while a purely functional monarchy is perhaps a contradiction. We can defend monarchy in terms of its utility but in the end its appeal lies in the way it relates the present to the past and personalizes society and nation.

Queen Elizabeth's Golden Jubilee will be in 2002. She is said to have been deeply affected and touched by the national celebrations of 1977 but 1992 must remain a bad memory. The Way Ahead group has identified the Golden Jubilee as an opportunity to stimulate and demonstrate public affection for the Queen and the monarchy and detailed arrangements are already being made for it. The Queen Mother must hope to live to participate in this jubilee and, if she does, it is likely that, not only will it mark fifty years of the reign of a monarch, but also homage to a family whose sense of duty commands enormous respect. Four generations from Queen Mother to Prince William are more than most families can muster but even three will demonstrate the human continuity that is at the heart of the institution of monarchy and that a family at the head of the state is still, as Bagehot put it, 'an interesting idea'. Monarchists will hope that the Golden Jubilee will see an appreciation of monarchy as an organic concept that enables a society to relate to its past achievements, while, by its capacity to evolve, it can strengthen the bonds of a rapidly changing culture and continue to enable the individual to feel part of a collective whole far more effectively than can the transient authority of elected politicians.

Notes

Introduction

1   *The Twilight of the British Monarchy*, 'an American Resident', 1937, pp.13-14.

2   G. Orwell, 'As I Please' in *Tribune*,
    24 January 1947, printed in *The Collected Essays, Journalism and Letters of George Orwell*,
    1970, vol. 4, p.317.

3   See Edward Shils and Michael Young, 'The Meaning of the Coronation', *Sociological Review*,
    vol. 1, No. 1, 1953; N. Birnbaum 'Monarchs and Sociologists: A Reply to Professor
    Shils and Mr Young', *Sociological Review*, vol. 3, No. 1, 1955; J.G. Blumler, J.R. Brown,
    A.J. Ewbank and T.J. Nossiter, 'Attitudes to the Monarchy: Their Structure and
    Development During a Ceremonial Occasion', *Political Studies*, vol. 19, No. 2, 1971;
    S. Lukes, *Essays in Social Theory*, 1977, R. Coward, 'The Royals' in
    V. Beechey and J. Donald (eds), *Subjectivity and Social Relations*, 1985, David
    Cannadine, 'The Context, Performance and Meaning of Ritual: The British
    Monarchy and the 'Invention of Tradition' c. 1820-1977', in E. Hobsbawm and T.
    Ranger (eds) *The Invention of Tradition*, 1984, p.104.

4   J.C.D. Clark, *English Society 1688-1832*, 1985, pp.161-5; see also James Lees-Milne,
    The Last Stuarts, 1983, pp.4, 5, 112 and 145.

5   Cannadine, *op.cit.*, p.109.

6   We are most grateful to Mr Stephen Broadhurst for this information and for
    allowing us to read his unpublished M.Phil. thesis 'Royalty and *The Times*',
    University of Essex, 1986.

7   See John and Jennifer May, *Commemorative Pottery*, 1972, Chapter 2.

8   W. Bagehot, *The English Constitution*, 1867 (1963 edn), p.85.

9   I..R. Christie, 'George III and the Historians – Thirty Years On', *History*, Vol. 71,
    No.232, June 1986, p.219.

1: George III

1   Cannadine, *op.cit.*

2   *Ibid.*,p.116.

3   John Brooke, *King George III*, 1972, p.85.

4   *Ibid.*

5   John Clarke, *The Life and Times of George III*, 1972, p.32.

6   Cannadine, *op.cit.,* p.117.

7   Brooke,op.cit.,p.215 and Frank Prochaska, *Royal Bounty*, 1995, p.12.

8   Brooke, op.cit., p.253.

9   Linda Colley, 'The Apotheosis of George III: loyalty, royalty and the British nation, 1760-1820', *Past and Present*, 1984; see also Linda Colley, *Britons*, 1992, pp.195-226.

10 Frank O'Gorman, 'The Recent Historiography of the Hanoverian Regime', *Historical Journal*, Vol. 29, December 1985, pp.1015-16.

11 Colley, *op.cit.*, p.111.

12 John Sykes, *An Account of the Rejoicings, Illuminations etc. etc. that have taken place in Newcastle and Gateshead*, 1821, p.6.

13 N. McCord, *North-East England*, 1979, p.101.

14 James Woodforde, *The Diary of a Country Parson*, 1758-1802, 1984, p.355.

Chapter 2: George IV and William IV

1   P. Ziegler, *Crown and People*, 1978, p.17; J.H. Plumb, *The First Four Georges*, 1974, p.171; Cannadine, op.cit., p.109.

2   Plumb, *op.cit.*, p.180.

3   I.R. Christie, *War and Revolution, Britain 1760-1815*, 1982, p.295.

4   John Stevenson, 'The Queen Caroline Affair' in John Stevenson (ed), *London in the Age of Reform*, 1977, p.119. Stevenson provides a first-class account of the Affair.

5   *Ibid.*, p.117.

6   H. Reeve (ed), *Greville Memoirs*, 1875, vol. 1, p.99.

7   H. Maxwell (ed), *The Creevey Papers*, 1905, vol. 1, pp.338 and 341.

8   H. Twiss, *The Public and Private Life of Lord Chancellor Eldon*, 1846, vol. 2, p.19.

9   M. Beerbohm, 'King George IV' in *Works of Max Beerbohm*, 1896.

10 L.J. Jennings (ed), *The Croker Papers*, vol. 1, p.196.

11 Cited in C. Hibbert, *George IV, Regent and King*, 1975, p.209.

12 Twiss, *op.cit.*, vol. 2, p.52.

13 Cited in Frank Prochaska, *Royal Bounty*,1995, p.43.

14 Twiss, *op.cit.*,vol. 2, p.72.

15 Hibbert, op.cit., pp.249-50.

16 R. Mudie, *A Historical Account of His Majesty's Visit to Scotland*, 1822, p.17.

17 Mudie, *op.cit.*, pp.104-6.

18 Hibbert, *op.cit.*, p.255.

19 R. Fulford (ed), *The Greville Memoirs*, 1963, p.27.

20 J.G. Lockhart, *Memoirs of the Life of Sir Walter Scott*, 1838, vol. 6, pp.360-61.

21 Duke of Buckingham and Chandos, *Memoirs of the Court of George IV*, 1859, vol. 2, p.419.

22 R. Huish, *Memoirs of George IV*, 1830, vol. 1, p.1.

23 Plumb, *op.cit.*, p.177.

24 P. Ziegler, *King William IV*, 1971, p.152.

25 Fulford, *op.cit.*, p.177

26 Sir G.O. Trevelyan (ed), *Macaulay's Life and Letters*, 1889, pp.176-7

27 M. Brock, *The Great Reform Bill*, 1973, p.198

28 C. Hibbert, *The Court at Windsor*, 1964, p.230

29 Ziegler, op.cit., p.157

30 *Ibid.*, p.294

Chapter 3: Victoria with Albert

1   E. Longford, *Victoria R.I.*, 1964, p.60.

2   R. Fulford (ed), *Greville Memoirs*, 1963, p.120.

3   S. Weintraub, *Victoria*, 1987, p.101.

4   Earl of Malmesbury, *Memoirs of an Ex-Minister*, 1884, vol. 1, p.95.

5   Newcastle MSS, 11 October 1837.

6   A.C. Benson and Viscount Esher (eds), *The Letters of Queen Victoria, 1837-1867*, 1908, vol. 1, p.156.

7   *Ibid.*, p.162.

8   *Ibid.*, p.174.

9   *Greville Memoirs*, p.155.

10 *Ibid.*, p.171.

11 *Ibid.*, p.160.

12 M. Wynn Jones, *A Cartoon History of the Monarchy*, 1978, p.90.

13 C. Hibbert, *The Court at Windsor*, 1964, p.257.

14 Weintraub, *op., cit.*, p.172.

15 A. Briggs, 'Prince Albert and the Arts and Sciences' in J.A.S. Phillips (ed), *Prince Albert and the Victorian Age*, 1981, p.66.

16 *Principal Speeches and Addresses of H.R.H. the Prince Consort*, 1862, p.112.

17 *The Letters of Queen Victoria*, vol. 2, p.5.

18 Malmesbury, *op., cit.*, vol. 1, p.345.

19 J. Buist, *National Record of the Queen's Visit to Scotland*, 1842, pp.4 and 22-31.

20 C.E. Quarme, *A Narrative History of the Visit of Queen Victoria to Lancaster in 1851*, 1877, pp.4 and 35.

21 Cited in J. Richardson, *Victoria and Albert*, 1977, p.133.

22 Malmesbury, *op.cit.*, vol. 1, p.319.

23 *Greville Memoirs*, p.233.

24 Cited in I. Gilmour, *The Body Politic*, 1969, p.315.

25 Weintraub, *op.cit.*, p.234.

26 *The Letters of Queen Victoria*, vol. 3, p.5.

Chapter 4: Victoria without Albert

1 G.E. Buckle (ed), *The Letters of Queen Victoria, 1862-85*, 2nd series, vol. 1, p.9.

2 E. Darby and N. Smith, *The Cult of the Prince Consort*, 1983, p.1; S. Weintraub, *Victoria*, 1987, pp.303 and 306.

3 *The Letters of Queen Victoria*, 2nd series, vol. 1, p.35.

4 R. Blake, *Disraeli*, 1966, p.747.

5 *The Letters of Queen Victoria*, 2nd series, vol. 1, p.102.

6 J. Cannon, *The Modern British Monarchy, a study in adaptation*, 1987, p.12.

7 *The Letters of Queen Victoria*, 2nd series, vol. 1   p.244 and pp.295-6.

8 Cannadine, *op.cit.*, pp.118-19.

9 P. Magnus, *King Edward VII*, 1964, p.101-2.

10 *The Letters of Queen Victoria*, 2nd series, vol. 1, p.255.

11 *Punch*, 7 July 1866.

12 T. Cullen, *The Empress Brown*, 1969, p.19.

13 B. St John Nevill (ed), *Life at the Court of Queen Victoria*, 1981, p.74.

14 W. Plower (ed), *Kilvert's Dairy*, 1870-79, 1977, p.166.

15 D. Thomson, *England in the Nineteenth Century*, 1950, p.171; Longford, *op.cit.*, p.391; Weintraub, *op.cit.*, p.371.

16 T.H.S. Escott, *England: Its People, Polity and Pursuits*, 1879 (1885 edn), p.350.

17 *The Letters of Queen Victoria*, 2nd series, vol. 1, p.379.

18 Magnus, *op.cit.*, p.17.

19 Malmesbury, *op.cit.*, vol. 2, p.294.

20 Longford, *op.cit.*, p.375.

21 T. Cullen, *op.cit.*, 1969, p.129.

22 D. Hudson, *Munby, Man of Two Worlds*, 1972, p.111.

23 Cullen, *op.cit.*, p.22.

24 Weintraub, *op.cit.*, p.3.

25 E. Hammerton and D. Cannadine, 'Conflict and Consensus on a Ceremonial Occasion: The Diamond Jubilee in Cambridge in 1897', in the *Historical Journal*, 24, 1, 1981, p.144.

26 F. Thompson, *Lark Rise to Candleford*, 1973 edn, pp.239-40 The wide range of goods advertised by using Victoria's name or picture during the period of the 1887 Jubilee is examined by Thomas Richards in 'The Image of Victoria in the Year of Jubilee', *Victorian Studies*, Autumn 1987, pp.7-32.

27 *Celebration of Her Majesty's Jubilee*, 1887, p.51.

28 W. Bagehot, *The English Constitution*, 1867 (1963 edn), p.95.

29 Longford, *op.cit.*, p.549.

Chapter 5: Edward VII

1 E.F. Benson, *King Edward VII. An Appreciation*, 1933, p.214.

2   *The Times*, 23 January 1901.

3   Giles St Aubyn, *Edward VII. Prince and King*, 1979, p.14.

4   Kinley Roby, *The King and the Press and the People*, 1975, p.32.

5   St. Aubyn, *op.cit.*, p.149.

6   Longford, *op.cit.*, p.315.

7   Philippe Julian, *Edward and the Edwardians*, trans. Peter Durnay, 1962, p.141.

8   St. Aubyn, *op.cit.*, p.146.

9   Roby, *op.cit.*, p.127.

10 *Ibid.*, p.245.

11 W. Bagehot, *The English Constitution*, (1963 edn), p.96.

12 Prince Von Bulow, *Memoirs, 1903-9*, p.386.

13 Cannadine, *op.cit.*, p.135.

14 *Ibid.*

15 For a discussion of the appositeness of 'renovation' as opposed to invention in this context, see J.C.D. Clark, *English Society, 1688-1832*, 1985.

16 A. Hyman, *The Gaiety Years*, 1975, p.32.

17 K. Rose, *King George V*, 1983, p.75.

18 A.J. Meyer, *The Persistence of the Old Regime*, 1981, p.137.

Chapter 6: George V

1   J. Stevenson and C. Cook, *The Slump*, 1979, p.276.

2   Harold Nicolson, *King George V*, 1952, p.5 George V has been fortunate in two of his biographers. Harold Nicolson and Kenneth Rose have both written highly readable and sympathetic accounts of his life.

3   *Ibid.*, p.40.

4   Kenneth Rose, *King George V*, 1983, p.57.

5   Nicolson, *op.cit.*, p.38.

6   *Ibid.*, p.14.

7   *Ibid.*, p.52.

8   Rose, *op.cit.*, p.36.

9   Nicolson, *op.cit.*, p.51.

10 John Pearson, *The Ultimate Family*, 1986 and David Cannadine, 'The Petticoat Power of Windsor' in *The Sunday Telegraph*, 20 July 1986.

11 Francis Watson, 'The Death of George V', *History Today*, December 1986.

12 John M. MacKenzie, *Propaganda and Empire*, 1984, p.92.

13 John M. MacKenzie, 'In Touch with the Infinite' in John M. MacKenzie (ed), *Imperialism and Popular Culture*, 1986, p.181.

14 *Propaganda and Empire*, pp.3-4.

15 R. Roberts, *The Classic Slum*, 1971, p.142.

16 M. Harris, *From Acre End*, 1986, p.67.

17 *Imperialism and Popular Culture*, p.169.

18 J. Richards, 'Boys' Own Empire' in John M. MacKenzie (ed.), *Imperialism and Popular Culture*, 1986, p.141.

19 Rose, *op., cit.*, p.174.

20 E. Longford, *The Royal House of Windsor*, 1974, p.21.

21 Rose, *op.cit.*, p.174.

22 Nicolson, *op.cit.*, p.335.

23 Rose, *op.cit.*, p.212.

24 Nicolson, *op.cit.*, p.63.

25 Longford, *op.cit.*, p.77.

26 *Ibid.*, p.94.

27 Nicolson, *op.cit.*, p.334.

28 Rose, *op.cit.*, p.393.

29 M. Muggeridge, *The Thirties*, 1971, p.268.

30 G. Orwell, 'The English People' in *The Collected Essays, Journalism and Letters of George Orwell*, 1970, vol. 3, p.33.

31 J. Pope-Hennessy, *Queen Mary*, 1959, p.598.

32 Rose, *op.cit.*, p.312.

33 *Propaganda and Empire*, p.88.

34 Nicolson, *op.cit.*, p.525.

Chapter 7: The Sons of George

1   M. Middlebrook, *The First Day on the Somme*, 1976, p.300.

2   HRH The Duke of Windsor, *A King's Story*, 1951, pp.187 and 192.

3   *Ibid.*, p.136.

4   R.R. James, *Memoirs of a Conservative*, 1969, p.19.

5   HRH The Duke of Windsor, *op.cit.*, p.287.

6   Cited in C. Warwick, *Abdication*, 1986, p.90.

7   HRH The Duke of Windsor, *op.cit.*, p.256.

8   M. Bloch (ed), *Wallis and Edward*, 1986, p.130. For similar views concerning their relationship, see: C. Warwick, *Abdication*, 1986, p.81; F. Donaldson, *Edward VIII*, 1974, p.108; P. Ziegler, *King Edward VIII*, 1990, chapters 13, 16 and 20.

9   J. Pope-Hennessy, *Queen Mary*, 1959, p.574.

10   Script of Gaumont British newsreel no. 271, 3 August 1936.

11   J.E. Wrench, *Geoffrey Dawson and Our Times*, 1955, p.343.

12   Lord Beaverbrook, *The Abdication of Edward VIII* (ed. A.J.P. Taylor), 1966, p.31.

13   R.R. James (ed), *'Chips', The Diaries of Sir Henry Channon*, 1967, p.89.

14   HRH The Duke of Windsor, *op.cit.*, p.385, for the role of the press see Lord Beaverbrook, *op.cit.*, p.68.

15   Lord Beaverbrook attributes this remark to Lord Kemsley, head of *The Sunday Times*, *ibid.*, p.66.

16   M. Davie (ed.), *The Diaries of Evelyn Waugh*, 1976, p.415.

17   Lord Beaverbrook, *op.cit.*, p.17.

18   The Duchess of Windsor, *The Heart Has Its Reasons*, 1956, p.252.

19   J. Stevenson and C. Cook, *The Slump*, 1979, p.276 and F. Donaldson, *op.cit.*, p.409. Diana Mosley, in her book *The Duchess of Windsor*, 1980, p.207, claims the number was 60,000.

20   The Commentator, 'Newsreel Rushes', World Film News, vol. 2, no. 4, cited in A. Aldgate, *Cinema and History*, 1979, p.139.

21   K. Middlemas and J. Barnes, *Baldwin*, 1969, p.1017.

22   J.E. Wrench, *op.cit.*, p.348.

23   Gaumont British script no. 308   Newsreel no. 308, with a special supplement 'Our New King and Queen', was first shown to the public on 10 December, the day on which Edward signed the Instrument of Abdication.

24   *British Newsreel Issue Sheets*. Complete collection held by the Slade Film History Register. British Universities Film and Video Council Microfiche.

25   J.W. Wheeler-Bennett, *King George VI*, 1958, pp.293-4.

26   E. Longford, *The Royal House of Windsor*, 1974, p.139.

27   *The Diaries of Sir Henry Channon, op.cit.*, p.463.

28 HRH The Duke of Windsor, *op.cit.*, p.258.

29 H. Jennings and C. Madge, *May The Twelfth*, 1937, pp.5 and 13-17.

30 J.E. Wrench, *op.cit.*, p.359.

31 J. Pope-Hennessy, *op.cit.*, p.575.

32 I. McLaine, *Ministry of Morale*, 1979, p.92.

33 J.J. Wheeler-Bennett, op.cit., p.470; cited in A.J.P. Taylor, *English History 1914-1945*, 1965, p.493.

34 N. Nicolson (ed.), *Harold Nicolson, Diaries and Letters, 1939-45*, 1967, p.100.

35 J.J. Wheeler-Bennett, *op.cit.*, p.429.

36 M.O. 1392, 25/8/42.

37 S. Briggs, *Keep Smiling Through*, 1975, p.69.

38 Lord Moran, *Diaries*, 1966, p.372.

39 M.O. 141, Report on Newsreels 29/5/40, and M.O. 2190d, 4/12/44- 30/4/45.

40 J.J. Wheeler-Bennett, *op.cit.*, pp.467 and 636-7.

41 M. Thornton, *Royal Feud*, 1985, p.4.

42 M. Frayn, 'Festival', in M. Sissons and p.French (eds), *Age of Austerity, 1945-51*, 1964, p.341.

Chapter 8: Elizabeth II

1 John Pearson, *The Ultimate Family*, 1986, pp.50-51.

2 Edward Shils and Michael Young, 'The Meaning of the Coronation', *Sociological Review*,
vol. 1, No. 1, 1953.

3 Dermot Morrah, *The Work of the Queen*, 1953, p.40.

4 Pearson, *op.cit.*, p.71.

5   Kingsley Martin's *The Crown and the Establishment*, 1962, epitomizes this analysis.

6   John Osborne, *Encounter*, October 1957; Lord Altrincham, *National and English Review*, August 1957, Malcolm Muggeridge's article 'Royal Soap Opera' appeared in the *New Statesman* on 22 October 1955, but it was his elaboration of his arguments in the *Saturday Evening Post*, 19 October 1957, which attracted attention and outcry.

7   Robert Lacey, *Majesty*, 1977, p.268.

8   Pearson, *op.cit.*, pp.172-9.

9   Some confusion still exists as to what the family name is. Princess Anne was married as a Mountbatten-Windsor, but when the Prince of Wales married his entry in the register bore no surname. The terms of the 1960 declaration were thus broken, with the Queen's permission, at the time of Princess Anne's wedding and the intention may well be to have a dynastic name, Windsor, and a family name, Mountbatten-Windsor.

10   There are many syrupy biographies of the Queen Mother. Penelope Mortimer's *The Queen Mother*, 1986, on the other hand, presents a picture of a female Machiavelli.

Chapter 9: Adulation and Obloquy

1   Andrew Morton *Diana, Her True Story. In Her Own Words*, 1997, p.204.

2   Philip Ziegler, *Mountbatten*, 1985) p.687.

3   Penny Junor, *Charles, Victim or Villain*, 1999, p.133.

4   See Penny Junor and Sally Beckhill Smith, *Diana in Search of Herself*, 1999.

5   Andrew Morton, p.203.

6   Ross McKibbin, 'Mass Observation in the Mall', *London Review of Books*, 2 November 1997.

7   Robert Lacey, 'The beatified and the damned', *Sunday Times,* September 26, 1999.

8   Julie Burchill, *Diana*, 1998.

9   Beatrix Campbell, *Diana, Princess of Wales: How sexual politics shook the monarchy*, 1998

Conclusion

1 Penny Junor, *Charles, Victim or Villain*, 1999

2 Frank Prochaska, *Royal Bounty, The Making of a Welfare Monarchy*, 1995.

3 Vernon Bogdanor *The Monarchy and the Constitution*, 1995, p.299.

Index

155